Your Right Action Number

\#

Juno Jordan

DeVorss Publications

ISBN: 0-87516-287-8
Library of Congress Catalog Card Number: 79-50006

Fourth Printing, 1998

DeVorss & Company, Publisher
P.O. Box 550
Marina del Rey, CA 90294

Printed in The United States of America

Acknowledgment

During the late 1950's, a numerologist and counsellor from New York City presented me with a new method of character analysis, not in common use at that time. She asked me to test it. It was called the PERSONAL YEAR.

As the new method gave so much insight into the nature of the experiences of my clients, and proved so invaluable in giving advice for "Right Action," year by year and month by month, I presented it to The California Institute of Numerical Research, Inc. for further development.*

Over a period of 25 years, year after year, each member presented (from living statistics) the results of his or her study and analysis. We proved, without a doubt, the accuracy and dependability of each year's instruction for Right Action for both material and spiritual success and happiness, especially when faced by life's continuing problems.

*The California Institute of Numerical Research, Inc. has completed its study.

The "GENERAL TREND" for each Personal Year is the joint determination of the Research Group. The "COMMENT" represents my personal evaluation and experience, gained from 50 years of consultation and teaching.

Foreword

This book is a numerology specialty. It explains human relationships for young and old. It solves personal problems; brings harmony between husband and wife, children and parents; assists business associates; and inspires cooperation between employer and employee.

It promotes dreams and aspirations, and at times right action for all endeavors.

It envisions opportunity month after month, year after year, even far into the future.

Numerology proceeds from the concept that all life, all form, known or unknown, is produced and shaped by the creative movement of universal energy. As this energy moves, it takes form as the wind, the sun, the moon, the ocean, the land, and all physical embodiments. From this form and the name describing it, the numerologist interprets its individuality, its purpose and obligation. As the scientist describes H_2O and interprets its qualities, in the same way the numerologist describes John and reveals his life and character. *Your* name and date of birth represent your *share* of this universal energy and reveal your chosen purpose in life. You, too, belong to the Heavenly Spheres.

Contents

Your Right Action Number

The Personal Year:

Its Right Action Nine-Year Cycle

THE RIGHT ACTION NINE-YEAR CYCLE

Every individual, young and old, has a Personal Year number. Your Personal Year number is hidden in the numerical statement of the month, day, and year you were born. Its influence continues on, year by year, throughout your lifetime.

As you begin to meet life's experiences, (to do and dare) and to reach out for opportunity to make a success of your life, your Personal Year number acts as a timing device, to channel your efforts and undertaking toward Right Action, thus avoiding what might otherwise bring failure or unhappy experiences.

These experiences are *timed* within a nine-year cycle of events. There is a beginning and an ending (timed) in each cycle. These nine-year cycles are repeated many times during a lifetime, accounting for the changes and unexpected happenings which may even re-organize a well-planned life or endeavor.

As you become aware of this accurate and continuing timing device in your affairs and are guided by it, you will gain a sense of being in command of your life and personal affairs. Self-confidence will be gained; surprising events will become opportunities, making what might have seemed impossible before, a stepping stone towards accomplishment and success. Your character will be strengthened and your new self-confidence will enable you to help others, wisely and well, adding usefulness to your endeavors.

Each Personal Year with its Right Action instructions is a constructive impulse towards opportunity and awakens again your inner desire for success and happiness in its timing.

Naturally, events must have time to unfold. As each Personal Year, within the nine-year cycle, has its special determination for Right Action during its period of influence, *each month* has its timing and Right Action also, progressing, in correct order, for accomplishment during the twelve months of the year. A Personal Year for everyone begins when the bells ring out on New Year's Eve, continuing until December thirty-first at the year's end. During this period of influence the Right Action for the year has its opportunity for accomplishment. It times the action, gives the opportunity to plan ahead and to be prepared for what other people might do to interfere with your plans. Your Right Action number will *prepare* you for unexpected circumstances, and at the same time alert you to opportunity year after year and month after month.

YOUR PERSONAL YEAR IN YOUR DAILY AFFAIRS

Suppose you were driving your car down a public highway and saw a red lantern in the roadway. You would be instantly alerted—Danger Ahead! and probably slow down, drive cautiously or stop to investigate.

Your Right Action number in the same way, takes notice of the signposts along the highway of your human experience and adventure. It says "Stop-Look-Listen!" It is a signal for Right Action and like the red lantern, is a guide for a safe journey, success and happiness along your pathway of life.

Facing the challenge of human relationships, day by day, month by month and year after year is not easy. Many problems come up: divorce, separation, loneliness, business failure, strife, drop-outs, competition, lack of opportunity, and misunderstandings. At such times, it may seem there is no justice, no place to turn for help, advice or assistance. But when you know and make use of your Right Action number you have a "signal" to guide you; to help you make decisions; when to move forward; when to wait; and how to act under the demanding circumstances.

Example:

A smart young man, making good in his profession, discovered a short-cut in the procedure of a national business company. He wanted very much to have it accepted by a group of professional men who were owners of the business. With an overabundance of self-confidence, he presented his plan and, as he said afterwards, felt he was going "to put it over on those wise guys". *He failed!* His timing was off. He did not know *his* Right Action number. He went in the spirit of a Number One Year—aggressive, self-determined, dominant and forceful, instead of being guided by his own Personal number at that time, the number *Two,* which called for tact, diplomacy, cooperation and *persuasion.* He had an unhappy experience which affected his business life and position in the world, simply because he failed to respond to his Right Action number. This often happens to those who plunge into experience without consideration of the proper timing. So much emotional and mental unhappiness, failure and misunderstanding could be prevented by accepting the information the Right Action number is prepared to give.

LET'S TALK IT OVER

Life would be beautiful, at least now and then, if people were not so hard to get on with.

Very often the problem is as much our own as it is of those who seem to be against us. This is mostly because the majority of people do not understand the rules for human relationships which are the basis for harmony and happy companionship. The guidelines which the Personal Years present, if followed year by year, will solve many of these problems and make for happier relationships between yourself and others.

For example, consider the relationship of a man and wife. She is in a Six Personal Year;* he is in a Seven Personal Year.** She feels the domestic influence which the Six Year exerts and which is her guideline for growth and development for the time being. She naturally thinks of the family. She has a sense of duty and the urge to make life happier for the family, children, and loved ones. She feels a desire, too, for love and approval from her loved ones.

She remarks to her husband, "Our wedding anniversary is coming up soon. Let's have the family and children in for dinner or a barbecue and a real get together."

He being in a Seven Personal Year, the spiritual year of his Nine-year cycle, would rather be alone than in the midst of family fun and gaiety, even though he

*Six Personal Year, Page 97.
**Seven Personal Year, Page 113.

loves his family. He says to her, "Must we? Let's go away somewhere by ourselves to a quiet place this year and be alone together."

How is this problem to be solved? Who is right? Who must give in?

The problem of getting on together continues. Next year, he is in an Eight Personal Year.* She is in a Seven Year, similar to his last year. He feels the urge to get ahead in business, to reach out for new opportunities. There are likely to be business conferences, meetings with important people, and it is necessary for him to be up and doing. He wants her to dress up, go places with him, and help him make an impression.

But this year she is released somewhat from many of the duties and responsibilities of last year. She does not feel like going places or mixing with the crowds which make up business interests and activities. She would rather go to an educational talk, or have time for quiet interests of her own. She says, "You go. I think I will stay home this time." In his disappointment, he goes alone. He may even take his secretary.

And so it goes. Unless they understand the reasons for these differences, year after year, the relationship may end in broken dreams, a drawing apart, or even in a divorce court. However, by talking over these differences, realizing that they are not real, only a personal timing for each one, a deeper understanding can result with a greater respect for each other. In fact, more fun and happiness will color their lives together.

*Eight Personal Year, Page 133.

Different number vibrations each year or even year after year should not be a real problem. The differences can add interest to an association, even to a business partnership. For two people to always think alike could result in boredom, and even create an inner desire for more life or new interests and contacts. Often though, two people who are not deeply in love have a pleasant and useful life together when their Personal Years are the same.

At the first of each year, greet it with the satisfaction of *knowing* what is expected of you, and all year long be glad you know and understand why certain experiences come to you and what to do about them. Be glad, too, that you know how to handle them. Allow your character to mature and your interests to expand, whether you are a business man, an artist, a housewife, or have a career all your own. You were given these guidelines when you were born.

FAMILY AFFAIRS

The training of children is made easier when the Personal Years are taken into consideration. The generation gap is far too often due to the lack of knowledge and understanding that a child's needs and aims are influenced by the number of his or her Personal Year.

After one of my lectures on the Personal Year, a woman said to me, "Dr. Jordan, you just saved my life. I am in a Four Year* and I was just about to land on my son with full force. Now I know better, I know how to manage. Thank you so much."

Children, on the whole, like to be disciplined, and this should be part of their training every year, but the *way* this training is given is the secret of a happy relationship. This mother, in her practical Four Personal Year, was concerned with order and system. She was stern and determined, more so than at other times, and was about to demand that the child do as she said. Her child might have been in a Five Personal Year, keen for life, experience, and excitement, resentful of being held to routine and practical results. He would want to be more free, to do the things he wanted to do, to get out with the crowd. This freedom withheld could only bring resistance and argument. This could be overcome by talking it over or simplifying tasks from time to time. To have insisted that he be punished for lack of application and failure to do his work would surely result in lack of understanding and a separation between mother and son.

*Four Personal Year, Page 67.

There is always a way to work out these differences. To know why these personal feelings and opinions exist, is a stepping stone to harmony and progress. Therefore, in training and disciplining children, it is very important to know what influences *you* are working under as well as *their* Personal Year vibrations and natural responses. Life will be beautiful and people will not be so hard to get on with when you understand *their* motives.

CONDENSED INTERPRETATION OF THE PERSONAL YEAR

The following imaginary relationship to the growth of a plant will give you your first concept of your own development through a nine-year cycle.

A Number *One* Personal Year is similar to the *planting of the seed.* The promise of growth and reward.

Number *Two* Personal Year is the *waiting* while the seed is in the ground. Whether it is growing or will grow is a matter of faith and patience. Do not dig it up.

Number *Three* Personal Year is like the sprouting under the ground which is not apparent from the surface, but the creative force of nature is going on.

Number *Four* Personal Year. Suddenly the seed breaks through the ground. This requires *effort* and *labor* to get through the sod.

Number *Five* Personal Year. From now on the plant grows and grows—a time for *moving forward* and progressive action.

Number *Six* Personal Year. The promise of a good crop as the plant flowers and is beautiful. Good care is now needed—*duty* and *responsibility.*

Number *Seven* Personal Year. The blossoms fall off, the fruit is small and green and should not be eaten. *Faith* is again required, and inner development. Soul growth is important.

Number *Eight* Personal Year. The marketplace and the time to display your wares and produce, *to get results.*

Number *Nine* Personal Year. The end of the cycle. The work is done. Be glad. *Forgive* and *forget* and get ready to let go for love's sake, and to begin again.

FIGURING YOUR RIGHT ACTION NUMBER

Before reading further, figure your own Right Action Number (Your Personal Year). Then get the *other* person's number—your business associate, your boss, your husband or wife, sweetheart or lover, your children, your in-laws.

Always reduce all sums to a single digit. A digit is the final addition of the component parts of any given group of numbers until a single number is reached.

Important: do not use your year of birth, but only the current year. Add the number of the *month* you were born, to the number of the *day* you were born, to the number of the *current year*. Reduce this sum to a single digit. This will be your *Personal Year* or *Right Action* Number.

Examples:

Take this group of numbers: 213
add these numbers together: *Two* plus
one plus *three* equals *six.*
(2 + 1 + 3 = 6) the single digit.

or 1974, a group of numbers: Add together
One plus nine plus seven plus four
(1 + 9 + 7 + 4 = 21). As this is not a
single digit; continue to add:
(2 + 1 = 3) The single digit for 1974.

Therefore, if you were figuring your Personal Year for 1974, and you were born October 9th, you would add 1 + 9 to the 3 of that current year. Your Personal Year Number would be 4.

(1 + 9 + 3 = 13) As this is not a single
digit, continue to add:
(1 + 3 = 4). This is your final number.
   Your Right Action number for that year, from January through December would be that of a 4 Personal Year, regardless of the day of your birth, early or late in the year. This does not change the face of the year's current calendar.

MONTHS

January	-1	July	- 7
February	-2	August	- 8
March	-3	September	- 9
April	-4	October	-10 or 1
May	-5	November	- 11 or 2
June	-6	December	- 12 or 3

To find the *Personal Month:*
   Add the Personal Year Number to the Calendar Number of each month.
   You are now ready to read what your Personal Year indicates and advises. Relate it to all of your personal affairs.
   You will be surprised and astonished at how it reveals what you are doing and what you *need* to do.

Number

1

Right Action

Your Personal Year Guidance

From January 1st to December 31st

NUMBER ONE PERSONAL YEAR
RIGHT ACTION

General Trend

Y OU ARE NOW entering one of the nine-year cycles which shape your life and encourage your progress throughout your lifetime. It also tests your character as a human being and makes you ready for the next round of human experience.

The feeling and desire to move forward, to improve situations, to do something about present conditions, to get on in the world, will influence your thoughts and desires. This is a natural urge, both material and spiritual. It is your Right Action motive all this important year from January through December.

Life never remains the same for long. Otherwise there would be stagnation instead of progress and humanity would die on the vine. If you are not aware of a desire, a sort of inner unrest, or need to improve something in your situation or environment or even your character, at least become alert to what is going on around you; otherwise you may be taken by surprise to find circumstance has acted for you.

It is advisable to overhaul your way of living. Make an effort to put your best foot forward. Take up a hobby or activity that will freshen your thinking and broaden your general activities, now, during your Number One opportunity.

19

The events of the year are not unnecessarily world shaking nor do they completely change all that you are doing, unless you want them to, or plan for them, but they do indicate that now is the time for improvement, advancement, and a new grip on your undertakings. The new cycle is a push forward, and to prevent you from getting in a rut!

People unconsciously begin to grow old, or let down a little when they fail to recognize this "beginning again". Life then slowly passes them by.

Be determined, if you have new plans and desires; but move forward wisely and consider all undertakings carefully. They can only work out gradually as the twelve months of the year pass by. Your Number One Personal Year is like a crossroad. You stand between the old and the future. The future depends on you. Look ahead, take a stand in your mind at least. Do not be impulsive, for there are many decisions to be made, month by month, before you can fully accomplish what you started to do when the year began. Reach out for the new opportunity.

Comment

The Number One Personal Year is a "renewal" year. Everyone needs something new from time to time. "Change is the watchword of progress." Possessions wear out and need to be repaired, renewed, revamped or remodelled, requiring time and planning. This is part of living. It is especially so during this "beginning year." Even our characters need remodelling. This may be true for you too, when your self-confidence, self-esteem, courage, energy and faith in the future are tested by Right Action now.

A Number One Personal Year is not an easy year. It is a very active year and there will be many decisions to make. Other people will be involved and there will be many things to be taken care of before the final plan is fully revealed.

To an active person, these may seem to be the ordinary run of daily events. To another, living a carefully organized life, events may seem like problems. It is according to one's way of life that events occur. It is only when we try to hold on to people, situations and possessions above all else, that the unexpected can disrupt the present way of life. The Number One personal year is a good year in that it renews opportunity, quickens the spirit of doing and keeps life moving forward. Make your activities worth-while to others as well as yourself. Rewards come in this way.

During the early months of the year, it is advisable not to be hasty, impulsive or too determined against all good advice. Progress now depends on you and your ideas, but others have an interest too, and must be considered. You may think they are holding you back, but remember now is a good time for planning. During the first part of the year, health matters of the family or associates could demand time and attention, when you are preparing to do other things. Take this as part of the delay of the moment, avoid resentment or anxiety. Worry or strain could affect your own health. In the Spring your plan should begin to get under way or to be more defined, bringing much duty in May. Take time out in June to think things over and seek advice and inner guidance by not being over anxious, as ideas may need time to set down roots. This is not a time to force issues. Many results will begin to come to a head in August and by December you will be at work on the plans of the year.

During the year, select these colors in flowers or decorations: flame, lilac, copper, and crimson.

> In Business—get together with associates for business improvement
> In Marriage—encourage self-development
> Children—teach self-reliance
> In-laws—encourage a new interest
> Human relationships—be an inspiration to others

MONTHS

As the months pass by, keep alert to the trend of thought and action each month suggests. The results will be colored by your character, your profession, your personal desires and your Destiny, as shown by your name given you at birth.

January—A Number One Personal Year
As the year begins and the new cycle gets under way, a plan for improvement or an idea for change, will be in your mind, due perhaps, to the lessons learned last year, during the closing of your last nine-year cycle.

Your plan will be for improvement in your way of living, and in regard to your home and business affairs. You should make an effort to move forward, to get things going, mentally at least, even though the way is not entirely clear. It will take time to gain full agreement. Discussions with others may even give something to "Patch up" leading to delays. Right now is not the time to be over-anxious or too positive about what you want to do. Be willing to cooperate as to ways and means. This is only the first month of the year. Keep plans moving forward but look carefully into the details of your plans. Then, too, others may not live up to their promises (or not be able to) for the time being. They may need more time for adjustments. It may be well for you not to become too involved right now. You may want to make demands later on when a better understanding will benefit all. Take time out for social activities. Do not be too serious. Enjoy the challenge of this beginning month.

February—A Number One Personal Year

The inner struggle over what you should or should not do, will be felt deeply this month. Many of the old problems will still be there. Do not be afraid to move forward for general improvement. Join with friends in their inspirational interests. Friends are important for they will help you if you are interested in their ideas too. You will be sensitive and emotional in your feelings and not realize it, even inclined to assert your rights. Be firm and determined, but friendly; do not allow annoyances to show. Do not talk too much or out of turn in your enthusiasm for your own plans. Others may think you are foolish and headstrong. If you are friendly, along with good judgment, you will get a lot of help and find that the outline of your plan is getting clearer in your own mind. Impulsive, headstrong action could bring deep regrets. Buy something new for yourself, take a short vacation; give a party, and add inspiration and imagination to your work, for color and enjoyment.

March—A Number One Personal Year

This is a practical month. There is work to be done. Even though there are obstacles present and many things to do and take care of, if you apply yourself and manage well, you should get plans better organized for future action. Concentrate on them, even though they seem to be delayed. Family matters or present situations can make it hard for you, requiring much of your time. Apply yourself to your tasks. Attend to the necessary details. Keep your courage and do not give up your plan for progress, and you will get results and the opportunity to do what you want to do later on. Manage, organize in a sensible manner; take good care of the obligations at hand; they are important now. Avoid arguments and disagreements. Keep your disposition guarded. You could feel some disappointment due to what others are asking of you.

Health matters of associates or in the family demand care. Take care of your own health, diet and find time to rest. Being over-anxious will not change the "care" or the work you must do now. Do not be too serious. Be especially sensible and wise for a month or so. This is not a time for dreaming. It is a period of attending to the things at hand and the problems of others. "Quiet preparation" is the Right Action for March. Contracts and papers and practical arrangements concerning any plan or agreement or regarding your personal possessions should be taken care of patiently. Overcome emotions and resentment.

April—A Number One Personal Year

This will be a busy month; eventful and forward moving. Now is a good time to forge ahead with your personal plans. "Progress" is the Right Action motive for April. After the routine and practical duties of March, the freedom, now coming up, will seem like a new life, giving you more opportunity to do what you want to do, and could not give your attention to before. Even though many avenues of interest are opening for you, you are apt to feel an inner unrest and some uncertainty. This is likely to be against someone or something in the environment, which you cannot completely change all at once. Arguments gain very little and quarrels delay the progress of the month. They have a way of taking care of themselves when not made too important. Changes in living conditions or occupation may be made if desired. New contacts and new interests lead to new ways and means. Be prepared for surprises and the unexpected, testing your ability to adjust to them; and to bring out your resourcefulness.

Legal matters regarding the old should be given careful thought, and can be to your advantage if you are thinking straight. Freshen up your thinking, your home, your associations. Travel, meet people. Make this month a progressive one.

May—A Number One Personal Year

Responsibilities and duties, both in the home and business demand your attention this month. "Service" is the Right Action keynote now; willing service. Others need your sympathy and help. Fair play between you and those you love or work with will bring good results. In business, more will be gained through compromise and willing adjustment than through self-interest alone.

Your plans and interests need some adjustment but should be going along with promise of reward, if you have been following the Right Action instructions; even though you still need to stand for your ideals and to work with them as you planned.

However, your emotions and feelings about what is right or wrong, especially in regard to the actions of others, might lead to resentment and jealousy and to impulsive action, against your better judgment. Try to realize this and act from your heart.

Family duties and responsibilities, which you have not had before, ask for your help and time. Children and their needs, the home, the family, love affairs and friends or loved ones, all seek your advice and sympathy. Your warmth of character and gentle response will save much controversy, even separation. Do not allow these demands to confuse your mind; much of the feeling will pass at the month's end. This is a very vital month for you. Meet all issues squarely with understanding and patience. Money can be received, even though many duties bring much expense.

June—A Number One Personal Year

This month's Right Action is quiet self-analysis, even in the midst of many tasks. It may seem, at times, that your plans are getting nowhere and that there is too much uncertainty regarding what others should do. If you can, get away for a while to rest and relax; this would be helpful for you will gain very little now by being too forceful and determined. Be determined in your mind and heart, for you know what should and can be done; but think everything out in a spiritual way; that is, find time for reading, thought and meditation, rather than to talk too much or to make positive demands. Take up a study or an idea that gives you inspiration and inner uplift. Your state of mind is very important and it is up to you. Meet financial obligations and pressures as they come up for there will be help there from past endeavors. You will realize more fully next month, that some of this waiting was necessary and a test of your character. Do not say too much; avoid arguments and criticism. Observe and watch, with good business judgment. Look under the surface of legal interests to make sure, in your mind at least, that others are right and fair and that the arrangement coming up will also be to your advantage. Discourage moods or depression on your part. Rest, eat carefully and take time out to read and meditate. Results will be better if you do. Enjoy this sabbatical type of month.

July—A Number One Personal Year

Now take hold of your plans in a businesslike way. Good judgment is required in regard to your relationships with others and in taking care of the results you are now about to realize. You will be getting ready for action, and will feel a quickening of your spirit of determination and self-esteem. Action is the keynote and little will be gained by just drifting and waiting; do those things you have been thinking about doing, and help results get underway. Have self-confidence and do not look back. You may still feel strain about money or finances, but it pays to smile; for if you keep your head and are efficient and a good manager, you will succeed.

Push forward for this is a time to buy, sell or to re-arrange property matters, business activities and living conditions, affecting you personally. A move or change, possibly a business trip may be made or taken, although this may not be a very important part of the general improvement. A feeling of release may be felt due to your good management and organization. Meet friends. Old friends can prove interesting.

August—A Number One Personal Year

Many of the plans which represent the year's progress will come together this month, linking the past and the future. This should be pleasing, exciting and eventful. Long delayed results will begin to show a positive direction and the possibility of being accomplished, relieving you of the tension, anxiety and uncertainty at last. Agreements and understanding will clear the way for the association which this represents and the opportunities which go with it. This may be a clearing up of some uncertainty of the past.

Review your early determination to improve your surroundings and to gain the freedom you desire for more time for personal interests. Get things done that need doing. Think plans over carefully for you are likely to feel differently about your situation and future and to view it in a new light. You, yourself will have changed and should realize that patience and seeming delay was all part of the plan. Your character should be a little kinder and more understanding. Join with friends in humanitarian interests. Enjoy entertainment, art and beauty. Take up a study or interest that will broaden your outlook on things in general. Self-confidence, self-esteem and personal satisfaction should not be egotism. However, love and sympathy get the best results. The new direction will still need time to fully work out.

September—A Number One Personal Year

From now on, the new plan and association will take most of your time, energy and good will. It has a far-reaching scope. There is no longer the need to be so personally determined for much has been accomplished by your will-power, courage, decision and self-reliance. This development of inner power has been the test of your character, all during the year, and should be one of your assets now. However, more tact, diplomacy and cooperation will be required of you in the new relationship, for you will not be entirely on your own, as time works out the new activity and interest. You may have to wait for others to carry on. Even though you are continuing with your personal activities and there are many things to do, September may seem to be a quiet month. Find time to rest. You may feel tired after the mental strain of the year. Have your annual check-up. Health matters and those of family, even friends, need attention. If problems in arrangements come up, use executive ability to solve them; do not try to solve everything. Free yourself from past duties, that is, put them in order. Do not carelessly neglect the tasks or duties at hand. Your life and plans are likely to be greatly influenced by others or someone else to a large degree, so know what you want; understand what others are doing. Hold to your position, but have patience and make few demands other than good business procedure. Make use of the lessons in management you learned this past year.

October—A Number One Personal Year

Like the seed in the ground waiting to sprout, October is a waiting month; but a busy, active time and interesting; even though you have many tasks and details to attend to while you are waiting to know for sure how the program is to be finally carried out. There is not much you can do to speed it up, but you should have the satisfaction of knowing it is a reality. Those in authority are also working to produce results, by December, at least.

You are likely to be coming and going a great deal, due to social activities, with pleasant associations, clubs, study groups, entertainments and invitations, all to your advantage, for you need to keep in touch with people, to advance your own interests.

This month is not without annoyances. You may be surprised at what friends, neighbors or family ask of you without consideration. Keep your own counsel. The Right Action intention is to be diplomatic and courteous, without becoming too involved in any one interest, person or situation. You may make an interesting friend or renew a friendship along the lines of an old association. Give time to good management and organization of your way of living, to finish and clear up what is no longer necessary.

November—A Number One Personal Year

Your Number One Personal Year has had two purposes; first, to direct your affairs towards the future and general improvement, and second, to develop your character toward self-confidence and self-esteem in the midst of problems, challenges and often opposition. You should realize this now, as you take time for more self-expression and personal interests and to enjoy your accomplishments. There may still be unfinished business to take care of, demanding your executive ability, determination and strength of character, but otherwise, this is an inspirational and creative month. It is a time for more freedom and pleasure and to put more feeling into your personal interests and activities, ideals of your mind and heart. Cultivate imagination and color life for yourself and others with beauty, art and inspiration and the happier interests of being alive. Join with friends and associates in creative pastimes, lectures, the theatre, games and sports, encouraging you to happier states of mind and endeavor. Friends will be an interesting part of the month. Love affairs or the admiration of others add to the inspiration. You may meet friends or relatives you have not seen for some time. Buy needed articles, gifts, even shop for Christmas. Do not be extravagant, or go to extremes emotionally. Gossip and things said or done impulsively could upset the good the month has to offer. Enthusiasm for living is the Right Action motive for this month.

December—A Number One Personal Year

After last month, December may seem different as it is a practical period; a time to get down to work and to face all of the responsibilities before you. At the same time, you should be pleased that many plans and agreements have been brought to a head, and that the slow summer months are beginning to show results. There have been many uncertainties and problems and you should now be realizing the results of your decisions, especially those concerning your association with others. Contracts and agreements give the promise of progress and show the way plans are going to proceed; also the work you are going to undertake.

A few details may not be to your liking, but will turn out all right as they are worked out with careful and determined management. Economy and practical management are part of this month; all business, social and general circumstances require it, due to what you have to do and many expenses to be met. All this is the basis for Right Action as you enter your Number Two Personal Year.

Take care of your health. As you may feel tired after the year's uncertainty, guard your disposition. Add some of the inspiration you gained last month to your plans for Christmas. Make others happy. A spiritual realization may add a new sense of well being. Look back over the year and realize it has been good after all.

Number

2

Right Action

Your Personal Year Guidance

From January 1st to December 31st

NUMBER TWO PERSONAL YEAR
RIGHT ACTION

General Trend

THE RIGHT ACTION this year is quite different from that of last year. The self-interest, determination and initiative are no longer needed. Your purpose and steadfastness will still be underlying all that you do, but success and good results are obtained *now,* through diplomacy, cooperation and the unity established between yourself and those you are depending upon for results. In fact, all during the second year of your present nine-year cycle, agreements and harmonious relationships in business or human association depend upon a willingness to *share,* when mutual benefits are required. How well you work with others, in all associations, is more important than the results you are trying to get. Your future, in later years, will reflect what you do now. The need for tactful approach in all dealings or undertakings is vitally important, and the exercise of patience when *delays* seem to hold up results, is the background for ultimate success.

Even if it is part of your plan to bring about a separation from an established tie, for better circumstance or environment, meet the opinions of others in such a way that such action does not become a problem, even on your part. Resistance, condemnation or dominant demands bring unhappiness and perhaps, even regret. It is really your task, all this year, to keep peace in your mind and heart. Otherwise, you could be pressed, by others, into an ungracious action; feel subordinated and not in control of your plans and Right Action. There is a spiritual color to this year; the realization that peace of mind and good will in all activity is more important than all other ways and means.

There is a sweet note running through the year: Love affairs, weddings, pleasing companionship, good fellowship and lovely social events. New opportunity, new associations open the way to the personal expression that your Number Three Year has in store for you when you begin the third year of your cycle.

Comment

Your Number Two Personal Year will be a busy one, with endless demands on your time, so much so, that you may wonder how you will take care of everything. Even so, this year, in itself, is designed to be a wonderful one, often exciting with new interests, new contacts, group enterprise and surprises, all to try to help you make this year one of your best. It holds many promises, even if not fulfilled all at once. Your talents, perhaps, the plans you were working on, or your personal interests will bring about the offers and contacts of the year. What you can do for others, or have done in the past, will be the attraction; sometimes with a "thrill of accomplishment" or on the other hand, disappointments, when the Right Action understanding and cooperation are not a part of the proceedings. Think each idea out carefully. Consider the ultimate goal wisely. Estimate its future possibility in relationship to what you want out of life. Like the seed in the ground, and not ready to sprout, realize time is part of the result. In this way avoid the possibility of defeating the ultimate reward and agreement. Experiences are deep and often emotional. Even so, do not allow your feelings to cause you to act hastily or with condemnation. Move forward as circumstances demand. Keep a cheerful attitude of mind. Enjoy working with others for a useful cause. In this way you will realize, at the end of the year, that you are happier and that a big need or problem has been adjusted and has been worked out for mutual satisfaction.

Up to July, do not hurry results. Time is very important and things will seem slow. From then on, you should know where you stand and just what you are going to do, and by the end of the year begin to plan for more time for yourself, and your personal interests and progress.

During the year, select these colors in flowers or decorations: gold, salmon, garnet, prune and cinnamon.

> In business—talk things over, and get together
> In marriage—find interesting group studies
> Children—teach courtesy and good manners
> In-laws—be patient
> Human relationships—stand for peace

MONTHS

Direct your undertakings by the suggestions given for the month. Many of the following indications will

take place depending upon your character and the destiny you are born for, shown by your name at birth.

January—A Number Two Personal Year

Respond to the inner urge you are feeling to get down to work on a creative talent or ability you have neglected for some time. The desire for more self-expression and to follow your own interests is good and right and you should plan for it with determination, even though not able to act upon it fully, at this time. A feeling of inertia, or perhaps not knowing just how to go about it, may have caused you to neglect it. If you are not aware of this talent, take up a study that will give you more self-confidence and enjoyment through the feeling of doing something worth while. (Each year of every nine-year cycle has its Right Action requirement, but also carries a demand for character growth for maturity at the same time.) Friends are important this month, by their interest in you. Social activities will take time and should be enjoyable. Make new friends and enter into the entertainment. There could be unexpected pleasures or surprises in the association, and in the help they can give you. The expression of cooperation which the year holds, begins quietly this month.

February—A Number Two Personal Year

This is a very practical period. There is work to be done as the result of last month's creative ideas and plans, with many details to be attended to, because of the needs of others as well as your own, and your desire to get more order and security. Without this practical management, delays could come up to force you to be more efficient and careful in regard to your association and agreement with those who are part of your future. The work should be of interesting nature as well as practical; including contracts and papers to understand and take care of. Many small irritations, due to slow moving results, will demand patience and good disposition. Be sure you understand what others want as well as what you want. Take care of your health and that of family and friends. This necessity could be part of the practical needs of the month. Friends may still be enjoyed and a help and inspiration. However, in regard to your personal affairs, decide to go ahead with the plans you have in mind and meet the opposition with the Right Action of the year: courtesy, diplomacy, and cooperation. In this way, you place a practical basis for further progress and your own good.

March—A Number Two Personal Year

This is an active month. Routine may be broken up, due to so many things to consider, in regard to the changes or renewals you have had in mind regarding your environment, location, partnerships and personal associations. This is a period for new interests, new contacts and a good time to keep affairs moving forward. The unexpected may enter in to direct your plans. It is wise not to talk out of turn or to argue with annoyance. Cooperate wisely and take care of legal matters from the right side of the necessity. Otherwise opposition could be annoying and delaying. Be resourceful in planning and to get results; talk things over. Remember the theme of the year is peace in your own heart, rather than force, to win over the opposition. Take a trip, join in public enterprise, buy something new and make this a month of progress for yourself and in all associations.

April—A Number Two Personal Year

Duty and responsibility are required. You may be judged by how you meet these requirements. They appear in business, and especially in regard to home and family affairs and loved ones. A warm heart and sympathetic response to the needs of those about you bring you great rewards and more harmonious relationships. Lovely things and warm response will be the result of your own efforts to improve your surroundings and to be helpful to those who depend on you.

Clear up conditions which are no longer necessary or of use at the present time. You will gain peace of mind in this way. This could be a problem and not easily accomplished, if you have not cooperated with others with the true desire to bring about better understanding and desire for the good and rights of others. Some of the responsibility will have to do with doctors' bills, legal affairs, etc. Your character and what you ask of life and others is important again, even more so than before. Be kind.

May—A Number Two Personal Year

This month, you seem to be standing on a plateau, waiting, looking back over the past, not quite certain of the future. There is little you can do now to force any issue. Many conditions will be adjusted as the month passes and you may seem to be more alone, to enable you to think your situation through for a better perspective; even though you are still involved in the problems brought about by what others do or have done. The Right Action is to keep your poise and self-control. Avoid resentment if results are not just what you expected or wanted.

In one way, you will experience a sense of relief. On the other hand, a sense of regret may be in your mind; a feeling that others may have been unfair in what they have done, leaving you more alone.

May is a sort of sabbatical period. You really need time to rest, relax and quietly think out everything and control your moods and feelings. Even if you desire help and assistance for your future progress, do not try to look too far ahead at this time. Have little to say, even if finances are slow or uncertain. This is not the time for personal demands or for sensitive emotions. More is to be gained by an inner poise and strength. When you gain this, an illumination and inspiration will flood your being, clear up the whole situation and give you a new viewpoint and understanding of what is required of you. Regardless of creed, cult, religion (or no religion) review your own actions; how cooperative, kind and understanding have you been in the past? Be fair and help will come in surprising ways. This will turn out to be not only an important month, but a really happy one.

June—A Number Two Personal Year

There is not a lot to worry about this month. Your affairs will be gaining headway and you will feel stronger and more able to take care of your business and general affairs. It is possible to make improvements now and you should feel more peace of mind through activities planned and undertaken with the advice and help of friends. Changes in your way of living and in your associations may be under consideration, for business reasons. There may be something hidden or that you may not want to tell at this time. Just be efficient and use good judgment. Again, this is not the time for emotion or foolish sentiment. You should gain by what is done now, but keep in mind, there is an element of the temporary present and the need for cooperation is still present. A trip for business reasons, even for health and rest (even pleasure) may be made this month. You should realize easier financial conditions due to the help of others. It is up to you this month to be on the job, to go forward with what you want to do. At all times, *get good advice* from those who understand and have had business experience and are in good standing.

July—A Number Two Personal Year

This month brings the realization that an old association, activity or relationship is no longer a part of your life and that the patience and cooperation in regard to this is no longer needed. If you are taking this experience harmoniously, and with the realization that you did your best, then, when this month is done, you should move forward with deep self-confidence and a sense of relief, and find more time for pleasure, enjoyment and personal expression, based on this fulfillment. Try for an inner peace, even though at times, the past experiences have often been emotional, confusing and difficult. The Right Action this month is to be generous, forgiving and kind, allowing the past its freedom, as well as to claim it for yourself.

Up to this time, efforts to get results and Right Action from others, could only be accomplished through tactful and diplomatic approach, patience, and the consideration of the needs of others. Self-interest only, in all relationships, business or human relationships, meant opposition and delay. From now on, as this month is completed, you will be more free to go ahead on your own. Remember, cooperation is still the keynote. Finish up loose ends. Let go of that which is no longer necessary to your progress. Keep a warm heart, and think big, and your reward will come in its own way.

August—A Number Two Personal Year

As your Number Two Personal Year is a time for growth and development and time is necessary for final results, this month may seem a bit dull and slow. The many little things to take care of seem like inaction on the part of others. They could make you nervous and emotional and affect your health during the summer and fall of the year. Remember *time* is essential all year long. This is a growing year, like a slow-growing plant. Gradually, however, a new idea will be realized which will turn your attention to the future and to what you really want to do. As the month passes, you are likely to become aware of a new state of mind regarding yourself and what you want from life. This may be along philosophical and spiritual lines of thinking and feeling, perhaps coming as a surprise and not experienced before. An inner sense of enlightenment will subconsciously guide you as you get ready for a new start and new relationships in the future. However, give things time, for even with many adjustments made during the past months, and many improvements, small annoyances can come up in business affairs and human relationships. Discipline your thoughts, and refuse to act in any way that will force issues of the past and cause you regrets. In fact, this is another time when it is wise to watch your disposition and to be careful of what you say. Relatives and their problems may call for your ability to comfort and for diplomatic approach. A new association may be an opportunity and prove to be part of the growing interest of this month. Share what you know for mutual benefit and interest. Unity, one of the talents you have developed during the year, is still the Right Action. Have a purpose of your own as this year begins to pass, for your own self-development and happiness.

September—A Number Two Personal Year

In many ways, this month is the crest of the year's experiences. The real purpose of your Number Two Personal Year has been to show you the value of patience, under opposition; to demonstrate how satisfactory results can be attained through cooperation and tactful approach in all dealings without authoritative position; and the value of "diplomacy" for mutual benefit, rather than for self interests alone. Appreciate what you have gained. Keep a quiet, inner poise and enjoy this month. Engage in social activities. Take short trips. Join with friends and loved ones in their interests. Music, art and the cultural aspects of living, literature, craft, studies that bring inspiration and faith in the good in the world, are associated with a Number Two Personal Year. The changes the year has brought will lead to a decision about yourself. Progress and results, during this year, have depended a great deal upon *your* character. If you are the positive type, unyielding and personal where your interests are concerned, results may be temporary. Or if you are the sensitive, self-conscious type, others may have overlooked your interests. However, this year should have given you the opportunity to show your talents for cooperation, and given you more authority. The need for patience will be cleared away this month. Look forward to what you want to do next year. Your Number Three Personal Year (self-realization) is coming up in January.

October—A Number Two Personal Year

Now that unity has been established between yourself and those you are dependent upon or are part of your present situation, it is time to think about what YOU want to do, for more personal self-expression, in your own way and according to your talent and ability. Perhaps a trip or vacation or change of routine is in order.

Ideas, leading to future undertakings, perhaps different from what you have previously been doing, will begin to direct your plans (more for the future, than the present). What you feel about your future is important to you and should be carefully considered. However, your emotions are still sensitive, where others are concerned and need control and discipline. Do not talk too much about what you feel or think you would like to do, but join with friends or associations interested in self-improvement.

Friends will help to make this a pleasing month. Social activities will be attractive and take much of your time. This is a good time to attend lectures, take up studies and to appreciate art and beauty; all to stimulate a desire for a better expression of your own character and personality. Your living conditions and environment may seem different for a while but interesting and worth-while. Children can prove interesting and offer you an outlet for your emotions. Love affairs, the admiration of others could make this month very enjoyable. You have had many details to take care of this year and could be a little weary. Take care of your health. Reach out and take your place among those who add inspiration to each day.

November—A Number Two Personal Year

The Right Action this month is to get down to work, to face the facts of what must be done, to establish better order and management for future security, and to be willing to apply yourself to the task, even though you may not want to. Meet the necessity present with good judgment and practical methods. Engineer the inspiration and ideas of last month toward accomplishment and for tangible results, to clear the way for what you want to do next year, and more freedom next month.

Many details accompany the work to be done, perhaps more than you expected, but which have priority if order is to be established.

Study ways and means, economize if necessary to get results, and do not hurry; just get things done. You may not like the routine and application or some of the little tasks that try to cause delay; show what you can do and be conscientious in your response to what others may ask of you. This can be a very satisfactory month, on the whole, due to your efforts and those you are associated with. Think plans out with good common sense, especially in regard to papers, contracts and agreements and to what you want to do, especially if legal matters are involved. Take care of your health by not being emotional or resentful or worrying over the details. In this way, the freedom for future activity will develop and be realized. In-laws and children are part of the responsibility the month brings.

December—A Number Two Personal Year

This Christmas month will be an eventful one, progressive in action, a bit hectic, due to a variety of interests and many irons in the fire, all to keep you busy, coming and going, meeting many people and to give you a sense of freedom and self-confidence.

Exciting events and unexpected happenings, new contacts and friends, related to old friendships, could bring a change in your plans or at least your idea of, or approach to, what you want to do or are planning for your general progress and advancement in the future. Your deep desire for more personal expression and to make a better use of your talents, knowledge and skills will be the basis for this, and your Right Action is to weigh and balance this urge, rather than to allow it to be a sense of discontent. Be independent, but not aggressive. Avoid arguments or quarrels regarding circumstance or the involvement with others which may be annoying. Remember, you are still in a Number Two Personal Year and getting together in a spirit of cooperation is still important. Children, family or business associates may ask for your time and help. Be helpful, resourceful, but put them on their own. Take care of your health by not over-doing. Look back over the year and prepare to make use of the lessons you learned as you move forward into your Number Three Personal Year. The seed in the ground is getting ready to sprout, to be sure.

Number

3

Right Action

Your Personal Year Guidance

From January 1st to December 31st

NUMBER THREE PERSONAL YEAR
RIGHT ACTION

General Trend

THIS YEAR, THE third year of your present nine-year cycle, belongs to you, even though you are involved in the affairs of others. We are never entirely free from duty and responsibility. Other people take our time and need our help. However, now and then we have the right to think about our own affairs and what we want to do and about what seems personally important to us alone. Otherwise, we would never find our real selves, or discover our own true worth. Life would be dull if entirely dominated by the demands of others.

Your Right Action, during your Number Three Personal Year is to believe in yourself and the ideas you have been carrying in your heart and mind, but never expressed. At least dream about them. Dreams have a way of coming true in the most surprising way! Inspiration, imagination, creative thought and deep emotional feeling are all qualities of character that make people great, and give color and warmth to all levels of living, in business, art, entertainment, labor or the most practical field of endeavor.

Keep in mind that this is not a duty year for you, even if you have many tasks to take care of. Follow the strong desire for self-improvement, at least in some simple and constructive way. Find the time to do so, but think out the plan without too much emotion; this might cause you to act impulsively and extravagantly.

To be one's self and to dare to follow a dream, to even go ahead with the idea, does not mean to throw all standards to the wind, just to get your own way. In fact, this should be guarded against, for you are likely to be very sensitive especially about what people say, even unintentionally, and you could make mistakes. Self-development, however, should not be expressed as over self-importance.

This will be an eventful year, at the same time. Pleasure, travel, many social activities, friendly gatherings and entertainment take on color. Your best results will be attained through a happy mind. Love affairs, your own and those of others will give you much to think about, with overly deep emotional feelings, on your part.

Comment

As the years of each nine-year cycle come and go, (you will experience many nine-year cycles during your lifetime) each year presents its own special requirements and obligations. These are the basis for progress and are the quickening ingredients for success, happiness, and ultimate attainment as the years pass by. The experiences they bring, serve to develop your character and to fit you for future opportunity. They also subconsciously test and awaken your spiritual nature. They are to direct you to self-confidence and self-esteem and to your rightful place in the world.

This should be a very happy year. It is intended to be so, but depending on you and your *emotional* direction, your renewed sense of self-confidence, and the interesting activities you are now undertaking. At the end of the year, that which seemed impossible, in the beginning, should be accomplished, leaving you with the feeling of work well done and the year very worth while.

During the first part of the year, however, make sure your plans are well thought out. Even this inspirational and creative year must be planned from a practical and working basis. Resentment, arguments, jealousies, hard words, from friends or associates or even on your part too, should be quickly adjusted to avoid disappointment and delay. Renew your plan in your own heart. Do not feel at any time that you are put down or not given credit for what you can do; get good advice and instructions; have faith in yourself, but guard against hasty or impulsive action, for right here, your happy Three Personal Year could get off to a wrong start, scattering your energies toward regret, even inertia or *lack* of physical well-being. Friends will be willing to help you, if you are not lacking in consideration. At the same time consider their advice carefully for in their enthusiasm, they could lead you on a detour or wrong action, and cause delays both material and spiritual, before you get on the right track again.

If your life is well established and you do not feel the need of change, and especially if your work and way of living is routine, at least add fun and inspiration to the lives of others. Entertain, give gifts, (avoid extravagances, one of the scattering forces of the year) and renew your friendships. Study, read, attend lectures, and freshen your mental and creative faculties. Your plans for self-development should bring you popularity, romance, love and admiration. The eternal triangle may call for decisions, and emotional control. Do *your part* to make this phase of your life lovely. Keep your enthusiasm and your dreams. A spiritual enlightenment can come to you as the year ends to make it all worth while.

Colors to help you "win" this year: Rose, ruby, amber, russet.

> In Business—friends are important
> In marriage—take a trip
> Children—introduce art and beauty
> In-laws—be friends, buy them something
> Human relationships—be a good friend, make friends

MONTHS

Direct your undertakings by the suggestions given for the month. Many of the following indications will take place depending upon your character and the destiny you are born for, shown by your name at birth.

January—A Number Three Personal Year
Even though the year, as a whole, is one of inspiration and creative activity, this month is a very practical one. There are many things to do and to attend to during this first month of the year. A necessity of practical nature, is present, and it is best for you to concentrate your attention upon your present problems in order to gain better management and order. You may

be holding up something for others, and it is even possible that a friend or loved one may be causing you some emotional disturbance. If you get on the job NOW and are self-sufficient and determined, and do not quarrel or act emotionally, you can get hold of conditions for your own present and future advantage. Look underneath the surface and know what is best for all concerned; and then act upon it in a sensible manner. This is the Right Action for the future. Friends may cause you disappointment or difficulty unless you are aware of this problem. Try to get harmony and the right viewpoint. Avoid unhappy reactions and *too* much personal feeling.

February—A Number Three Personal Year

This is a very important month during your Number Three Personal Year. You may be feeling that too much depends on you. The inclination to act impulsively must be guarded against; unexpected happenings, due to others, come and go throughout this month. What you plan and hope for might not go forward just as you planned. This is a good time to make changes for advancement and more personal opportunity, but not from restlessness or over-confidence. Base your plans on practical considerations as well as personal desire. Do not *bottle* up your emotions; work them out in a constructive manner between yourself and those concerned. Children, young people, or family may be part of the problem. Do not quarrel, for at this time, haste, temper, or resentment could start you on a *detour* or delay, until well into the fall of the year. Do not talk too much about yourself. In fact, all this year, be careful of careless words and conversation which could prove to be a boomerang. Your Right Action is to keep busy and meet all surprises with resourcefulness and versatility. Wasted emotion could lead to accidents and delays or poor health. Changes are in the air to clear the way for your own general progress; plan for them. Apply yourself, do not wait for others to help you right now.

March—A Number Three Personal Year

As a result of the activity and new ideas of last month, it is now necessary to give time to getting everything adjusted and in its right place. This is essential on all levels of work, or endeavors, and in all considerations. Talk things over with others for better understanding, and for the good of all concerned; to be sure. Meet the obligations and duty with good will and a helpful spirit and get down to work. If you wish to adjust matters between others, or to break up some tie or relationship, this is a good time to do so, but be kind and helpful. In fact, personal obligations seem to be brought to a crisis by your plans, but others must be considered, even though this is *your* year. The way is there; you may not see it at first. Also this is a good month to pay up obligations, to make repairs, to buy clothing, and to do the necessary little things. Avoid resentments and, if the adjustment is made now, a friendship can be saved or an emotional upset avoided. Pleasant associations enter to make the month interesting as well.

April—A Number Three Personal Year

This month could be slightly trying unless you are wise, thoughtful and exercise self-control. You may feel that others are taking advantage of you and there is a need for poise on your part and deep consideration of the problem brought about by your personal decision. Others may be annoying, but you may also be confused and too emotional to think wisely right now. You may feel alone or hurt by what others do, but later in the year you will find it was unintentional, so do not make a mountain of it. Get the right basis for understanding, and keep out of the affairs of others as much as possible, for arguments and too much talk may make matters worse. There are unexpected gifts and nice things to be gained through inner realization and faith in life and yourself. Keep your own counsel this month. Think quietly and carefully. Watch and wait. Too much emotional feeling will bring negative results and cause health problems. Nothing is gained by forcing issues. Your Right Action is to think about what you want in life and hold to it.

May—A Number Three Personal Year

This is a business month, and as a result of the quiet thought and observation of last month, you can direct business matters for a new direction and improvement now. Business arrangements may be made even though there are financial conditions slightly trying or demanding good judgment. Executive ability and efficiency will help carry things through. This is no time to be emotional or over-optimistic, even though this is an optimistic year, for through lack of self-control or wise direction, you could lose the way this month, or get on the wrong track or spend more money than you should. Changes connected with business are possible. Take good care of your health by lessening your food intake and taking the right exercise.

June—A Number Three Personal Year

This month brings many things to a head. Up to this time you may have made an effort to do what you wanted to do without full satisfaction and with some uncertainty. But at this time you will realize that you are at the end of some work, task, or plan and find this ending of things a release in some way and an improvement in the end. Real estate and property must be considered in a businesslike manner, and there may be conclusions regarding this, leading to a completion of certain activities. You may be wishing to sell something, but time may be needed, although you should realize now that you are finished with some old arrangement, activity, association, or personal relationship. It seems best to let go of things no longer needed; this will be the best way in the end. However, it may be a few months before the final stage is reached, perhaps September or October. The feeling of release, may be an emotional improvement resulting in the realization of what you have accomplished the first few months.

July—A Number Three Personal Year

Life seems to be leading you in a new direction. You should find yourself more free to do as much as you wish to do, but still not able to see clearly ahead. At first, the way may seem a bit indefinite and uncertain; you may be troubled about others and what you seem to be compelled to do for them, even though you realize this is not your duty. You should be able to make a selection, at least momentarily, which will affect your future greatly and open a new way for yourself, even though it is not accomplished immediately. All circumstances are working toward better things, and if you will keep alert, have faith, and not worry or doubt, you will sense this, and know what to do at the right time. You may make a vital decision or have an awakening of some sort where your affections are concerned, even though you are not quite happy and feeling tired. The Right Action of the year's progress is being born and you should continue to make the effort toward inspirational and creative self-improvement. In fact, this is the keynote of the whole year, SELF-IM-PROVEMENT IN EVERY WAY. If you live in your personal emotions, without some constructive outlet, you may be unhappy and feel very much out of things. If you are friendly and have something to give to make others happy, there will be interesting contacts and much more harmony and good will in your associations and surrounding. Turn your deep personal feelings into good works. Do not bottle them up; take a trip, or visit someone, if possible.

August—A Number Three Personal Year

There are many little tasks to do this month. Details to attend to. You seem to be away for a time or going from one place to another. You are likely to be involved in the affairs of others in a way you cannot help, and patience is a virtue. If you give things time, you can find the way to set yourself free from some tie or responsibility which has been part of the year, carrying over from June, when you hoped to make the final decision. Associations can be dissolved or changed and new interests can be developed. Moves or changes in environment may take place, or be considered. Pleasant happenings through friends make the month interesting and help can be gained if needed. Attend to all matters patiently and be agreeable and cooperative. Social activities, you may be away or find associations different for the time being.

September—A Number Three Personal Year

This is also an important month. It is a time to plan for the future and to do the things you have wanted to do all year concerning your own opportunities and personal self-expression. A personal plan or determination can now be carried out and more fully realized. This may come about quickly through friends or avenues suddenly opening up. Plans relative to property, work, and future activity should begin to clear up, and right now the opportunity to go ahead is present, if you take the right mental attitude, an optimistic point of view, and are not afraid to move forward. Try to be happy. No matter what others say, do what you think is right for yourself and do not waste time in unnecessary words and talk. Get action now, even if others seem to be against you. You, yourself, may be highly emotional and easily upset because of the attitudes of those you love or are dealing with in business or social activities. Gain self-control for health's sake. Seek spiritual help and business counsel. Avoid negative thinking or blaming others. Engage in cultural activities. After all, a degree of self-satisfaction should fill your mind and heart now, because of what you have done and stood for all year. Your Number Three year has called for a happy state of mind because of your faith in yourself. Count your blessings, be kind to yourself and be glad that you finally managed as you planned.

October—A Number Three Personal Year

Practical matters come up again and the details of last month's inspiration and progress must be worked out. Now is the time to execute and carry out plans. Much responsibility is on your shoulders. Take good care to have all contracts and agreements in good order, and get the reins of practical control in your own hands in a wise, sensible, and practical manner. Look after your health now by proper diet and periods of rest and relaxation. Do not be too serious or intense, even though you must be practical. A reorganization of plans should be realized in some way, after the many periods of uncertainty which the year has brought. This may be necessary to place your work on a firm foundation for next year's accomplishments.

November—A Number Three Personal Year

This is a very eventful month. Friendships can be proved this month and next, and much help can come through those who love you; friends and relatives. An active month, giving more life, new interests, and progress. In fact, you now seem to have a new outlook on life because of the experiences of the year. Also, you seem to be realizing a pleasing freedom. Take advantage of the new things. Take trips or move, if you desire, and overcome nervousness. Friends of the past year can and will help again. And, while there are some trying things to handle, and *unexpected* happenings, you can gain advantage and obtain fine results. More public life and new people to meet. A good time to take up new interests and studies. Business should show an improvement in a satisfactory way through your own resourcefulness and progressive spirit.

December—A Number Three Personal Year

This is a busy month, but a happy one, due to your being able to help others and do things for them. You will have responsibility and be called upon to render service to others and find little time for yourself now, for from now on you will be getting into a practical year and will be compelled to put your ideals and dreams of the present year into form for more lasting results. The *culmination* of many things and many conditions will be settled at this time. You seem to be at home, or have your time taken up with affairs of family and relatives. So this is the month to be unselfish and to make others happy. You should be more settled in regard to the activities of September, even though you have much to talk over. Love affairs and emotional matters are to be considered and enjoyed. This is your duty month and Christmas time.

Next year opens with a more serious aspect, but simply to force you to be a good manager of your own affairs, and to give you the opportunity to show what you can really do.

Number

4

Right Action

Your Personal Year Guidance

From January 1st to December 31st

NUMBER FOUR PERSONAL YEAR
RIGHT ACTION

General Trend

Your NUMBER FOUR Personal Year is a year of opportunity. But it is serious in tone. It is one of the practical periods of your life and not a time for dreaming, personal indulgence or careless living. Your dreaming-time was last year.

This is a building year, based on practical values and the steady application to assure you the results of your labors. It is a time to think in terms of order, system, good management and economical procedure for a more stable and secure future. The progress of the year may seem slow, but time will be needed to place the firm foundation upon which your future depends. This is not necessarily a problem; it simply is one of those times in your life when it is up to you to know where you stand in life and to be practical about it.

All your affairs, living conditions, family matters and business activities should be given economic consideration to establish stability and a firmer basis for future growth and dependability. A lot of application and attention to details will be part of the daily and monthly requirements. You may not want to do this, or feel you have already done so over a long time, but it is likely circumstances will take a hand and make it worth-while to put a little more effort and system into even your social interests, for better relationships, peace of mind and happiness. If you do this, when the

69

year is done, you should have a sense of satisfaction and pleasure, because you accomplished what you set out to do. The end of the year can even seem like a transition from one level of living to another; a sort of change-over in your environment, emotional relationships and business conditions.

There will be times when you will be judged by your character and the way you take hold of things, your energy and good common sense. This is the Right Action that gets good results and more progress is made.

"All work and no play" is not the only rule of the year, however. There is fun in the year too. Social gatherings, meetings, parties, trips, combined with business are all part of the year's interest. Take part in these to make sure you do not become too serious as the year passes by. Relatives and in-laws call for your help and understanding. Health matters should be attended to as part of the practical management of the year. This is a good time for an annual check-up as part of the Right Action in your Number Four Personal Year. Lots of hard work, but necessary for your own satisfaction, is in order. A good time to buy, sell, build and exchange. Read the fine print of any transaction. Be sure.

Comment

Begin the year by asking yourself a few questions—to discover your practicality; how much order and system are in your basis of operation? You may not want to be orderly or economical. You may want to live carelessly or without restriction. However, there is a right time for everything in life and this year, according to the rule of Right Action, you could find that circumstances in your own life or even those of the world of business and your association with others, will cause you to estimate and appraise your ability and to formulate a plan of action for security, happier relationships and business advantage.

Do you know where your insurance papers, your mortgage or your lease papers are? Do you owe anything? Try to get it paid up. Do your budget. Live well, but do not neglect it this year. How much money have you; property, jewels, personal assets? In other words, for your own satisfaction, get down to bed-rock, upon which to build and stand and move forward. Do not be surprised if some things you had not thought of, come to the surface, to show you the way you should go or act, as the year progresses. An awakening to the facts of your life should in the end give you a lot of satisfaction.

During the year, select these colors: blue, indigo, silver, maroon and green.

> In business—work for good management
> In marriage—work together
> Children—discipline
> In-laws—help them to be self-reliant
> Human relationships—help others build a good life

MONTHS

Direct your undertakings by the suggestions given for the month. Many of the following indications will

take place depending upon your character and the destiny you are born for, shown by your name at birth.

January—A Number Four Personal Year

As the year opens, you will be thinking about doing a number of things or want to do them, but at the same time you are likely to be uncertain about the outcome and the way to go about getting results. However, what you decide to do greatly influences the rest of the year, although not fully apparent at first. You may receive practical offers and face opportunities, but make everything you do count toward the future rather than for the moment only. New ideas now may not be vital, only interesting but leading to more definite interests later on. You will have the desire to get things in order or settle down, but due to many irons in the fire or to some work associated with others, you may not be able to do so in any noticeable way this month. You are likely to have spurts of enthusiasm and lose it again, but as the month passes, you will strike a balance between desire, uncertainty, and endeavor. You may be nervous or uncertain or may be away from home or under different conditions for the time being, but by the end of this month or the first of next month, you will be more clear in mind. This may be, too, to get free of something or to get away from someone or some condition in order to give you the chance to do what you feel you need to do according to the instructions of the year. It will take some time to get everything worked out. A trip or change and social activities color this month. Nice things through friends are possible. Family responsibilities are part of the decision.

February—A Number Four Personal Year

This will be a very busy month because of the many things to be done and the plans you have in mind. Now you can get down to more conscientious work and to the schedule and routine which is part of the year's work. You are likely to realize more fully now that there is work to be done demanding patience, application, and attention to detail, if you are to get established or attain concrete results, which are necessary for peace of mind and upon which to build your future. There are obligations to be met which you cannot rightfully escape, and much work to accomplish, both inside the home and out in the affairs of business. It may seem to you that others are imposing on you or taking advantage of you, and this is probably true, but these difficulties can be adjusted through talking things over, facing facts, and placing the parts of the burden where they rightfully belong. Take a helpful attitude of mind, and try to harmonize situations, for this will save the association and friendship, too. Remember that this is your year for practical work and accomplishment and for digging in and doing what you know must be done. It is not likely that you will get too much inspiration, day by day. There are many nice things to be experienced during the year, but these come through your willingness to do the work and to meet the necessities of the moment. Family matters must be taken care of and relatives may begin to present problems, but do not take on more than is right or fair, even though you are helpful in attitude and willing to assist them; avoid resentments or hard feelings so as to prevent quarrels or arguments which get you nowhere.

Look after your health now as well as your finances—
that is, do not let small illnesses or troublesome conditions go without attention.

March—A Number Four Personal Year

As you know, there are right times as well as Right
Action for everything under the sun. March is one of
the important months of your Personal Four Year as so
much depends on whether you make a real effort to
understand what is going on as well as to understand
yourself. You will have the realization of a problem,
part of it your own and part of it belonging to your
associates. Health matters and finances enter into this,
and it is wise to take everything quietly, even though
you keep very busy. It is advisable to say very little and
to get away now and then to rest, relax, read, write or
study, for in this way, and through periods of meditation and deep thought, will you work things out well.
To be moody and difficult could upset the apple cart of
success and happiness for the rest of the year, especially
if you permit discouragement to enter in and also if you
refuse to meet the conditions present. Allow others the
right to their ideas and desires now to quite a degree.
Do not *argue* about anything or build up misunderstanding; take time to think conditions out clearly and
with peace of mind. Say a prayer and have a lot of
faith, for plans can work out better than you think
later, even though something is very irritating now.
You could quit something now, or feel like it, and in
many respects you will be more free to do what you
want to do. A lot can be accomplished in spite of little

problems if you go ahead with skill, discrimination, and executive ability. Affairs of relatives need attention and you may possibly sell something or plan to do so and turn this into an improvement. Do not be too serious, and take up a new study or mental interest for fun and inspiration to help you meet your practical needs.

April—A Number Four Personal Year

You will feel more free this month and more able to go ahead with the work or plan which is practically a necessity, if you are to get the freedom and the money you need and desire. You should feel happier, too, or at least be conscious of a mental release as the result of finding the way to manage and arrange your financial affairs, for the time being. This is a good time to buy, sell, or trade, and to put your mind to getting the things done which will put all your business, home, and family affairs on a better basis for management, use and security. There may be papers to sign and legal matters should be well understood; it is wise to make sure that all details concerning legal matters or agreements are in first-class order. The way may not be perfectly clear, even with some improvement, and there can be a problem about getting things done. Analyze everything carefully and keep a clear head, and be prepared for surprises or unexpected things which call for good management and first-class endeavor. This is no time to trust to luck or chance, for there is likely to be an undercurrent of opposition or possibly delay and this calls for your best business efforts. Good judgment, efficiency, and executive ability combined with good common sense are important now. Some things may not be fully accomplished, but advancement should be apparent.

May—A Number Four Personal Year

Plans should come to a head this month or you will reach a conclusion, and this will be about finishing something—a plan, work, or undertaking or association as the natural result of what you have been doing the past months. A decision to take up a new plan, work, or way of living may be the outcome of this and new ideas regarding the home, family, and business are likely to influence your thinking and have a marked bearing on the future. You may have to push a little to accomplish what you have planned. You could be conscious that some activity is not going along as rapidly as you wish. But remember that this is a slow-moving year, demanding work, routine, effort, and patience, and it may be the old arrangements need to be cleared up before the new can get under way. Finish what is at hand. Keep cheerful, generous, and helpful. Keep your chin up and your courage high, and be willing to work and share with others. Get together with others to get plans accomplished. Realize that much is shaping up even though the way is not too easy. Get things done so you will be free to go ahead next month. The end of old associations may be realized, or friends or relatives may go their way.

June—A Number Four Personal Year

Many things come to the surface this month and you

will be busy because of the decisions and plans of the past two months. It will be necessary for you to look well ahead and to be determined and definite about what you want and are going to do. The decision you are making now seems to be rather personal and you need to take care to get the Right Action and to make the right decision. Get the true facts and the true values, and do not be carried away by big ideas unless you understand them and have estimated your ability to carry them through. This is a time to look to the future in a very definite way. By now you should have picked up loose ends and adjusted old situations which have been holding you back or were unfinished. From now on you will be moving forward with your practical plans for more security and general improvement. Try to get the reins of your affairs into your own hands as much as possible in a businesslike way. Do not force issues without good judgment, but with energy and deep determination, bring about the order that is necessary to place the lasting foundation which the year offers. Economic conditions may be slow and demand attention, and a family crisis of some sort may be present or represent change, but the whole month should bring interesting experiences and opportunity. You can engineer affairs toward a good end if you keep on the job. Attend to your personal affairs wisely.

July—A Number Four Personal Year

Even though you are busy doing a number of little things, you seem to be waiting upon circumstances and upon what others are doing. A great deal of tact and diplomacy are needed, and if others seem to oppose

you or if you feel a little out of things and a bit subordinated, do not mind this, for time is needed to get
projects under way and for results to become fully
apparent. Older people and relatives need understanding on your part.

Do not try to hurry anything but have quiet talks
with those concerned, for in this way you will gain a
great deal of knowledge and receive the help that you
need. You could take a trip in association with someone
else, although this is not certain. However, there are
many social activities and new friends to make. You
may enjoy a picnic or parties and find children or
young people bringing pleasure or inspiration. By now
you probably have the reins of your endeavors well in
hand, even though you may not realize just how fully at
first. This month could be a *turning point,* and if by
chance you have just drifted along and not made a con-
certed effort, circumstances could bear down upon you
and force you to cooperate with others, without gain for
your future that could otherwise be present. This is a
very fine year in its possibilities (but it is not easy), and
you can enjoy it if you take a wholesome attitude
toward work and the needs of the year, and are willing
to take the necessary responsibility to help others.

August—A Number Four Personal Year

This is likely to be a very busy month. It is not as
practical as the past months, for a good many things
should by now be accomplished. In fact, August is the
best month of the year to take a vacation if you are
going to have one. There are still many practical

responsibilities on your shoulders and you still seem to have many details to attend to for others as well as for yourself, but these are not too serious. Try to get a little fun out of life at this time. Even though business affairs may be moving slowly, you should find an inspiration and uplift from money made from your efforts up to now, and some money could come easier than you expect. There is a release of some sort in this month to give you a feeling of happiness and cheer. You may take a trip or at least make new friends and be meeting people who will mean a lot to your future. Spend a little money on yourself, but do not be extravagant, and work out new fresh ideas of creative and artistic nature to add color and charm to your practical endeavors. Letters, lectures, and new ideas and interests are your Right Action objectives during this month, but be careful about talking out of turn.

September—A Number Four Personal Year

You are likely to be working very hard, and all your affairs of a practical nature should be right at hand for management and direction: property matters, business, family, and health matters all come up, but a move and culmination of duties and tasks show much improvement for more settled conditions. You may be surprised to find that you feel alone or out of things and that you are emotionally disturbed, but this is not really so. You have only made a change and brought things to a head. Refuse to let anything get you down. Get the lowdown and look back at what you have accomplished with satisfaction and thankfulness. Give yourself time to adjust to the new arrangement. Take a little time out, too, for the sake of your health. Eat properly and get enough rest, for you have been a busy person all year. Many arrangements have been accomplished, and if there are still existing problems, this is only because you must carry on with what you have planned and worked for all year. Your efforts have placed a background, a protection and a business opportunity for the rest of the year and for the future.

October—A Number Four Personal Year

This is an interesting and active month. It brings a thrill in the new interests, new work, new people, because of changes and eventful happenings which come up during the month. Old conditions will still prove to be interesting, even though you are in a new phase of life, mixed in with the old. You should feel pleased about the activity and the many interesting experiences. You may have more than one iron in the fire, so remember that this is still your practical and sensible year. Evaluate all activities or new interests for their real worth. Add a bit of color and enterprise to your work, and even though you have a lot of responsibility still present, get fun out of what you are doing; rise to the occasion if the unexpected comes up to test your resourcefulness and versatility. Much still depends upon you and your own efforts. Attend to legal matters in all dealings with others, and do not be hasty or impulsive in any dealing of a cooperative nature. This is only the beginning of what is to come and is the first touch of the activity of next year. Some of the interests of the moment may not be lasting, and there is still much to think out. You are going to be more free personally as the coming months unfold their tasks and duties. Look ahead and be progressive in spirit and interest. Avoid arguments and hasty decisions; these cause problems. Young people and children are part of the month.

November—A Number Four Personal Year

During this month and the next, you may feel a little weary and restless, and slightly uncertain about some of your plans. Your main affairs should be running along according to pattern and schedule, but someone or some condition may seem hard and annoying. The sensible thing to do is to take things as they come and leave a lot unsaid, especially concerning relatives or family differences. The need for money is present because of obligation in your home and business. Meet your obligations as they come and you will find things easier than you had expected. Worry is the wrong method or to be angry or out of sorts about things or people. You may make a decision about someone or a plan, and it may be well to keep it to yourself for a while. Do not be disturbed or give up if the way does not open up all at once. There are many nice things to be happy about concerning your home and family, so be a good fellow and a good sport in everything you do. You are still making an adjustment to activities you have not been used to; just keep the show going. Some of the plans and activities of the present time will work out more definitely next year. This year you had to make your start and set the pattern.

December—A Number Four Personal Year

This month is a time for quiet endeavor and for a quiet Christmas. Even though you seem to be the one who must be practical and look after others, this is not your duty Christmas, and it is best not to undertake too much entertainment, especially if you do not feel well. It is possible you may find money a little short this practical year. A slight feeling of humiliation may be experienced because of what others do, but some of this may be because of your own actions or thoughts rather than a reality. All month, keep your poise and avoid worry or a confused state of mind. Have a great big FAITH in yourself and in things in general, and a recovery and an improvement will come about making the year much nicer than you had thought possible. The month might begin with slow tempo, but it will be fine in the end if you are patient enough to let others help and not try to do too much yourself. Your whole life is now on a better basis, and this will gradually show itself as you go along next year. To talk too much is to waste energy. Give yourself a nice Christmas. Let life show you the pleasant rewards it can bring you because you are calm, patient, and not asking too much.

Next year will be a busy one, too, but will give you more freedom, based on the foundation you placed this year.

Number

5

Right Action

Your Personal Year Guidance

From January 1st to December 31st

NUMBER FIVE PERSONAL YEAR
RIGHT ACTION

General Trend

THIS YEAR HAS many things to tell you. It is a time
when new projects can be undertaken and when
new interests are likely to come into your life. The year
has a strong bearing on your future, as it is a year of
progress and growth and demands that you be alert and
"up-to-the-minute" as to what is going on in the world
of progress and opportunity. As the year opens, you
will sense, subconsciously, that new opportunities and
new conditions are in the air waiting to be taken advantage of. They may appear as changes, even as ups and
downs, or as the unexpected, which may come up from
time to time. You are again given the opportunity to
move forward, rather than to "stay put" in the old routine of last year, and to put your best foot forward for
general and all around improvement in your life-style.
The trend of events during the year is in the nature of
new experiences. Change of environment, new relationships, new ideas, and new contacts, new plans,
more freedom, more variety and enterprise, color your
affairs. These may not be drastic or difficult, just a
freshening of interest, even taking you into the public,
travel or group activity. Even so, the old is related to
the new and part of the progress. Your work will be to
relate the two for more success and a broader field of
interest and activity.

There is a worldly color to the year. You may find
that you are restless, wishing for more social activity or

some new outlet for your energies. You may feel tired of the old routine. This may cause you to be impatient, restless, with the desire to get rid of an old condition or circumstance. This should be avoided, for even if the year is one of new impulse and energy, it is not suggested that change should be sudden or hasty or that you "burn your bridges behind you," only to regret it later. There is nothing to be gained by running away. Take the old that you built up last year into the new undertakings for progress and wider scope of activity. Changes may take place, even though you are not inviting them, so look for the opportunity which is present when they come about.

Take advantage of the changes and the greater freedom and progress which is the Right Action theme of the year. You may begin something which will carry on through the year, even into the future, and be rewarded for your past efforts.

Comment

"Don't fence me in" is a strong characteristic of the Number Five Personal Year. The desire to "live," to have the right to come and go at will and to have something doing most of the time, is a subjective influence behind its force and decision.

Without the "do and dare" spirit of this number, life would be very dull and lacking in all progressive endeavor. It is the drive behind advancement and the incentive which gives an outlet for man's genius and which drives him into the new and unknown, even to partake of the unusual and impossible. Without this drive, mankind would stagnate.

There are two ways to respond to this urge to be up and doing. The first is to accept this inner drive; to realize it is a "timing" in your life—to add improvement to what you are doing in the way of variety, new ways and means, and to do it without disrupting what you have already established, rather than to tear down or quit what you have already done. It is a time to put more enthusiasm into your undertaking, with a new mental attitude; all of which will lead to new contacts, progressive activities and a new understanding of yourself. In this way, old conditions and problems will clear up of their own accord and beneficial changes will occur. The second way is to be impatient, restless, critical and unreasonable about past duties and responsibilities, with such a strong urge for more life and personal freedom that all discretion is thrown to the winds, leading to quarrels, disagreements, broken promises and accomplishing little. Instead, get a lot of fun out of the year. Show versatility in your interests, business, social and even spiritual concepts, which may come up for your consideration from time to time.

You will still find many things to take care of which you may feel tired of, in a general way, but do not be impulsive or hasty or head-strong when little annoyances seem to deter you; haste and irritation can side-track you. Confusion could lead to legal problems, hard to deal with because of the reaction of others. Good judgment is necessary now. Older people, children or those younger than yourself should be a source of inspiration as well as a care.

This year, if lived right, can be a marvelous year.

The changes, even if unexpected, can be thrilling and exciting. In the end, you will be satisfied with what you have accomplished and pleased about the changes.

Colors for your Number Five Personal Year should include: pink, cherry, claret and wisteria.

In business—advertise and add new projects
In marriage—find a public interest in common
Children—give more freedom, with trust
In-laws—do not ask them to babysit
Human relationships—public interests or progressive nature in world affairs

MONTHS

As the year passes by, direct your undertakings by the suggestions given for the months. Many of the following indications will take place—at least there is a tendency for them to happen and work out, depending on your character and the forces at work shown by your name at birth. People differ in their responses to life's pressures and individual destiny. Pick out the good and directional advice given for each year and month and keep a firm control over your affairs to prevent the possibility of the negative trend getting the upper hand. Following the advice for the year and the month will help you have confidence in what you are doing for the best that life has to offer for personal advancement.

January—A Number Five Personal Year
Some of the duties of last year are still present.

Adjustments in the home are part of the month's activities. You should be willing to accept the responsibility and talk things over with others for the good of those concerned as much as for your own good. A plan is going forward and, if it is not of your making, it will come through what others do. Changes are in the air. All during this year, again and again, you will meet problems or conditions which will need to be carefully thought through because of the pressure for change and improvement. You may not fully realize what this is at present, but may sense it because of what others are saying and planning. This is no time to quarrel. The duty is yours and must be accepted at this time even though you may feel you are forced to do so. Illness may be present and you may feel you have too many responsibilities for your own good. By the time the year is over, you will realize that great changes have taken place for greater freedom and progress. Be sympathetic and patient now.

February—A Number Five Personal Year

There is much for you to think out quietly, as nothing can be gained this month by demanding or forcing the issue or through too much talking. This is important. Instead, find time to be more alone, to meditate and be quiet. Consider your problem in regard to your future freedom. Use your head, and plan. Changes are impending and even though connected with some confusion, they are necessary for progress. You may feel a deep inner struggle; that you have been placed in the wrong light, or are limited financially. Guard your disposition and be thankful that you are relieved now of some of the duties of last month. Find time for rest, physically, take care of your health, and look after your diet, for worry will gain you nothing. Relief will come, unexpectedly, to help you do what is necessary. But, through lack of self-control, temper, and quarrelsome methods, you could make mistakes and delay the good which is running through the year. This is very important right now. Think things out to a logical conclusion, and do not be emotional; then this will be a good month.

March—A Number Five Personal Year

There is need of good business judgment in all undertakings at this time. Something demands change, perhaps in your environment or for more self-expression. If you have not realized this before, you will now, and now is the time to plan for action for more freedom and personal opportunity. Meet the opposition with genuine consideration. Even though there may be some mental confusion, or you may not see the way clearly, do something, especially about your problems and burdens of last year. Find the way to do what you know you must do, or at least try. Do not just let matters drift. You can gain help through others if you are businesslike and make contacts with those in authority or influence. Your finances should be a little better. But if you cannot make radical changes and get full results now, do not make this a difficulty, for there are things to be brought to a head in either April or May, before you can feel or see the new way clearly.

April—A Number Five Personal Year

Future conditions depend now upon how you get on with others. Others may be difficult, but avoid resistance and condemnation, for this would bring matters to a standstill. Endeavor to see things in a helpful light; look at both sides of the proposition to gain the best results. You may still feel some confusion and things may be disturbing to you because of the realization that old conditions are no longer satisfactory and must be done with. You may be able to bring affairs to a head now if you try. Take a stand, for it is possible to make an adjustment both within your mind and in practical matters. Even though you feel a bit disgusted about others, you can reorganize your plans, improve your health, and bring more satisfactory results where others are concerned. Many circumstances may seem trying for the time being, and you may be disappointed, but do not allow this to upset your plans, for next month you will see farther ahead and be able to plan more definitely. Refuse to quarrel or argue. There is a need for agreement which calls for *tolerance* and good will. Attend wisely to any legal matters. You could be away from home temporarily for a short trip, or find something different for a time, during this month.

May—A Number Five Personal Year

While changes are impending during the year, still, this can be one of the most interesting and exciting years you have enjoyed for some time because of the new things coming up from time to time and the surprising turn events take. New people to meet and new ideas to give a thrill and, during this month, something of this sort could appear. Some unexpected condition can work to your advantage if you manage well. Your mind should be more free, realizing a number of old problems have been cleared up and that better understanding has been reached. You can begin activities now which will carry into the future. So do not be hurried, but go forward, be enterprising, and work in a new direction. Others may cause you annoyance, but there is fun and pleasure in the month. There is a stand for you to take, but again, the warning—be constructive and do not allow little things to mar your good judgment. Your environment may still be annoying, or you may be wishing you were out of it or doing something different. Do not be too concerned over the opinions of others. Be progressive in your own way. Your mind should be more at ease.

June—A Number Five Personal Year

There is need of patience at this time. If you exercise this and are tactful and diplomatic, you can bring about fine results and realize a closer association which will be of benefit in the future. Do not allow delays to trouble you. This is a danger point here—to be too forceful may antagonize and waste time. Just be patient in little things, for there is not much you can gain for yourself alone, but more by helping and working with others. Work is necessary to carry out plans, for while results may not be apparent, there is much going on underneath the surface. In fact, this month could be a turning point, a test of character, as to how well you are handling the impatience you feel as others are difficult to deal with. Changes seem to take time, and too much drive brings delay and can upset the working out of plans.

July—A Number Five Personal Year

This is a good month for a vacation. Friends will help or some new interest may come through friends or friendly assistance. You may be conscious of an inspiration or an unexpected idea that can result in great improvement if you follow it up and use your head. Do not be too emotional, but it is a good time to enjoy what you are doing, to entertain, and to attempt to make new friends. Trips, studies, parties, and better things to come. Ideas now can lead to future interests and progress. Watch for the inspirational idea. Do something, too, for the sake of self-improvement. Do not let this month pass without making a creative effort. Not a serious month, and you could spend too much money if you are impulsive. But if you are progressive and alert to opportunity, you can direct your affairs with considerable profit and satisfaction to yourself.

August—A Number Five Personal Year

The desire for freedom, life, and progress, which has been urging you to action during the year is strong now. If you have not made a definite effort to do something worthwhile, you now come to a place where practical plans must be made to clear away the obstacles and to get things in better order. This is a month of preparations, and it is necessary for you to face the facts, take the responsibility, and do what is demanded to bring plans to tangible realization. There may be demands for money, and you may feel limited, may not like the practical problems, but if you make the effort, go after results, and make your preparations in a sensible manner, you will accomplish what you have been wanting to do for some time, and find satisfaction in what has been accomplished. Take care of your health. Meet all opposition cleverly and engineer your own problem. Preparations for future action are now at hand and must be taken care of.

September—A Number Five Personal Year

A change, giving more freedom and something definite, is now under way about your plans for the year. This is likely to be in regard to domestic matters or to living conditions and environment. If you have been wise, progressive, and not discontented during the year, you should realize that your life has taken on new color, that there are interesting new contacts, and much has been lifted from your shoulders. This is a good time to take up new things, to advertise, to make public contact, to move, and to make general improvement. You may even take a trip if you did not do so in the spring or summer. Others may criticize you, and the possibility of quarrels is still present because of annoyances having to do with the old frustrations. Just go forward in a constructive and wise manner, for you have set yourself free from some old condition or responsibility. However, you may find a new one entering in almost imperceptibly. You should have no regrets, based on the year-long urge to make a change in the environment as well as for more personal freedom.

October—A Number Five Personal Year

Duty is present as the result of the activity and changes of last month. There are obligations to be met, and you seem to be doing things for others and to be concerned with the affairs of the home or where your real responsibilities lie. Take it now and be helpful to others. Do not be imposed upon but assist those around you. People may ask favors of you. Pay them if you owe them, and be helpful, for this month does not give one much time for oneself. An emotional problem seems to be present, in spite of all you have done, but you seem to be prepared to take care of it in your own mind and in your own way.

November—A Number Five Personal Year

As the year has been a very busy one, it would be a good thing if you could take a rest and be alone for a time. Look after your health by taking time out to get away from crowds and too much running around. You may find that you are more alone and out of things to a degree, but do not consider this a problem, for you need to think things out quietly, consider what you have done, and plan to go ahead with the activities regarding the changes of the year. You may feel discouraged, simply because you are tired and more alone. This is not the real condition, it is mostly in your mind. Have faith, do not lose sleep or worry over what others are doing. Say nothing, let them work out their own affairs and keep your self-control. Avoid misunderstanding by trying to see things in the right light and, in this way, a deep realization will be gained which will help you to continue to take care of all your problems. If money is slow, do not worry, for things will turn out better next month. Silence is a good policy, as is quiet determination.

December—A Number Five Personal Year

Finances will be better and conditions greatly improved, especially if you did not strive or drive matters too hard last month. There should be more freedom and enough money to do what you need to do, and this Christmas month can turn out to be pleasant and interesting. Trips for pleasure and business may come about suddenly and with good judgment, you can accomplish all you had in mind to do last month. You should realize that the year has been one of great importance, and that you are now really free from many of the old problems as your Number Six Right Action Personal Year approaches with its domestic affairs and responsibilities.

Number

6

Right Action

Your Personal Year Guidance

From January 1st to December 31st

NUMBER SIX PERSONAL YEAR
RIGHT ACTION

General Trend

Y OU ARE NOW on the upward climb of your present
nine-year cycle. The results of your efforts, work
application and planning should begin to present themselves. A great deal of attention should be given to the
ways and means by which your results may be attained.
This will depend upon how you approach and work
with others. *Service* is the keynote to results in every way
and in everything you do. This is your *duty* year and
you should keep this in mind, in the midst of pleasure
or problems. Try to make all responsibility interesting
to yourself, and the demands upon you, a privilege instead of a requirement. In this way, warmth and good
fellowship will make everything worth while, with
many pleasing returns for your effort.

Your future depends upon your ideals, standards
and good will toward others and you will gain by placing these assets into the fore-front. Everyone, at some
time, faces these requirements, out in the world, as well
as at home, or among family and friends. In other
words, during this special year, to think only of your
own well being and personal desires, could bring disappointment and regret later on in your expectations and
hopes for success and happiness.

Working together for the good of all, is the foundation of all human endeavor. The physician, lawyer,
minister, teacher, soldier, housewife, shopkeeper,
father and mother help make life a thing of beauty, in

some degree at least, so as the year passes by, do not miss this opportunity to give of yourself, in some way, to make others happy. It will all add up to your advantage as "spiritual blessings" and financial success, with love and harmony to make life worth-while. Next year will be different. Now, *Service* is the Right Action.

Comment

This year is a test of your character in a special way. You may love the home and family and its cares and responsibilities; or you may not. But this year cannot bring its reward, unless you meet the duty that will come up of its own accord in business or play.

There is a *care* running through the year which may bring expense and bills to pay. Even so, the opportunity for better financial returns are present to take care of the needs. This should be a pleasant year, with good nature and cheer in the midst of things which must be attended to. It is the nature of the year to bring love, good will, admiration, appreciation and pleasing relationships to all, if it is allowed to do so. However, it is the emotions—your own or those of family, children, loved ones, at work, or in social association—that may cause misunderstandings or difficulties. Feeling is strong as to what is right or wrong, leading to arguments, quarrels and separations. All year, justice, fair play, and honesty are important. Lack of truth and justice could bring legal problems, separations, discord, even involving children. Matters of home and property may come up for better management, more love and warmth of feeling and good will. This year, problems will be solved as you are the teacher, physician, psychologist, the mother, father and lover all in one.

The health of others may call for time and attention. Take care of your own health too; do not work too hard, and find time for rest and relaxation. Others do not want you to labor, just to help.

It may be September before you are free from some of your present duties. Do not say too much in October. So much will be clear as you prepare for your Number Seven Personal Year.

This wonderful year often means weddings, romance, reunions, communion with children, gatherings, celebrations with old remembrances and traditional standards.

Colors for Right Action Trends include: orange, henna, scarlet, heather and heliotrope.

> In business—service is the right way
> In marriage—equal rights
> Children—teach ideals, fair play
> In-laws—be kind and truly helpful
> Human relationships—humanitarian activities

MONTHS

As the months pass by, keep alert to the trend of action each month represents. The events will be according to your character, desires and destiny, as shown by your name given to you at birth.

January—A Number Six Personal Year

This is an important month for it shapes the future and holds so many promises, but on the surface you may not see this, and instead, feel held down or limited. You may also feel that others are opposing you. You are likely to be worried about your family or about health matters—your own or those of someone else—which foreshadow a real responsibility during the year. Things may not be as bad as they seem; your desire for improvement and accomplishment will be behind this feeling. You may wish to make the move or the change which has been your plan for the past few months and which you feel is a necessity. The prospects for accomplishing everything are good, but probably not now, and it is wise to do a lot of thinking and observing to make sure you get the right idea and do not make mistakes or cause opposition. You will get a surprising lot of things done if you push ahead quietly, but with poise, tranquility, and good judgment. If plans seem blocked, do not worry, give others time and opportunity to act on their own. Be patient and with good nature. To lose this now might upset the whole trend of the year. Before the month is over the whole way can clear up and with the help of others, you will find yourself making the change which seemed so impossible at first. Rest, relax. Do not talk too much about your plans.

February—A Number Six Personal Year

This month will be very busy; business and money management call for organization and efficiency. You will find help or assistance coming your way and a great deal to consider regarding houses and property. There will be much expense, but this will be managed and friends or associates will help. A lot of inspiration and fun can come from the activity even though there is much to do. This is the result of the planning of last month. Do not be extravagant now, for there is a lot of money to spend all during the year, and you should keep your eyes on the expenses and budget. You could have a strong impulse to throw common sense to the winds. It is all right to indulge in moments of grandeur now and then, but on the whole, the year is slow moving, with many demands for time and money. You will need patience and executive judgment based upon experience, past knowledge, and the true value and worth of things you dream about. Right now, however, you are going to be very busy, and there is the possibility of a business trip and the meeting of old friends.

March—A Number Six Personal Year

There will be many ends to gather up during the month, with the culmination of many things. However, do not rush ahead too swiftly; get fun out of doing the things at hand, for the slow-moving tone of the year will be apparent. You seem to be between the old and the new and to be wondering how to manage both; how to finish up some phase of the old, and at the same time, add new color, interest and business success to your undertakings. Add something new to your wardrobe, keep an even temper, be charming and in the midst of the many things to do. You can make new friends and enjoy old ones who will help make your duty year interesting. Young people may enter in, bringing duty but pleasure too. You are likely to be highly emotional or find yourself involved in emotional affairs, your own or of friends. Avoid being dominant and possessive in the midst of your success. Keep alert for new opportunities and lay hold of helpful new ideas. Something is likely to be completed which is a relief to you, and you may feel tired, even though a bit excited. Health matters seem ever present, but need not be too pressing, and it is a good thing to get some rest and to give your own health the once over. Tolerance is important now—*sympathy and broad understanding*—for resentments have a way of creeping into the Number Six Year, and if they take root, they upset the apple cart.

April—A Number Six Personal Year

Many things of different nature enter into this month. There is an idea you can catch hold of, or it may be just an old one that comes to the surface. This is the time to take action and to move forward, to do the things which are necessary to bring the improvement the year promises. There will be a lot to do. Some pushing is needed to get the ball rolling. You will be busy making arrangements to better manage your present opportunities. There may be a few air castles floating around, so to avoid plans not taking tangible form later in the summer and fall, outline a blueprint of action and be sure to get off to the right start. Overcoming moods is a good way to assure this. There is

a demand this month for you to know what you yourself want in your relationship to others, and to face
and accept the duty and responsibility which is part
of the dream or vision. Adjustments are likely to be
part of the month's experience, and again harmony
and good will are important. Do not take on too much
responsibility now in your desire for improvement.
Estimate and appraise again the worth and value of
everything now and in the future. You may have many
irons in the fire, interesting and instructive, all keeping
you busy.

May—A Number Six Personal Year

There are many things to do now, much responsibility and duty, all required to keep things going along
smoothly. This is no time to let down, and if you keep
an inner enjoyment for each duty and task, the month
will pass quickly, even though more time is still needed.
The advantage is now through cooperation with conditions, people, and yourself. Now is a good time to have
a discussion with relatives and associates for better
order in little things, but do not allow your disposition
to be mean or cross. There is much going on under the
surface, so take a quiet look into details of plans and
know what is what; assert yourself to a degree, tactfully, for something may not be presented in its right
light. On the other hand, by knowing the fine points of
all undertakings, you may be able to turn things to
your advantage and gain pleasing results. Surprises
may come relative to others or through what you hear
about others. This may not be vital, only interesting

and not too important. Know what is being done and *why*. Money conditions should be more settled. There is the possibility of being too easy going in your hopes and management. Social activities and public interests enter in.

June—A Number Six Personal Year

This is a good time to take a vacation. Some of the routine and slowness of the year can be lifted a little now. This is the one time during the year, when you do not have to think so seriously of your duty and when you have the right to do things which interest *you* personally and give you inspiration. A time for a trip, to entertain or be entertained, and to indulge in creative and artistic work. Attend lectures and do things at home and abroad which have to do with qualities of the soul and spirit; add inspiration to the lives of others, too. Spend a little money on yourself, but not too much, for very practical matters come up next month. You will be happy in some way, even though the duty is present. Live up to your own ideas and ideals now, for these seem to be important. Conserve your energies and be careful of what you say, for talk and gossip could mar some of the month's experiences. You may hear things, particularly about children or loved ones; the full truth should come out now or early next month. You have the opportunity now to present ideals to them or to teach, protect, and advise. Be busy about this in some way during June. Be willing to be told or advised for better understanding. The Right Action trend this month is for opportunities to go into business and to make more money. Financial reward is possible, so use good judgment now and be willing to work for it as you enter into July.

July—A Number Six Personal Year

This is a practical month, and you will realize this before the month is over. There is much to be done, and you may even feel you are a burden bearer. Apply yourself to the task and show your ability to manage. Assistance comes from getting good order, and applying to those who know, or are higher up in power or authority. Honors or recognition are possible because of your good work. You must get the work done and see things through with economy and good management. Hard work will bring good results. There may be something different this month in that living conditions are changed, or you may be away from home or living under somewhat different conditions. You may be doing work or be interested in things you have never thought of before. Economic conditions are present, at the same time, but on the whole, results should be pleasing and you should sense or begin to realize that the foundation has been placed for more money and financial improvement now and later in the year. Be careful of what you eat and of digestive upsets, and it is possible that money can be spent for health matters during the month. Do not work too hard, for *your* health and the health of those you love are important. You may meet people who may bring future benefits not thought of now, who will help you, and whom you may enjoy. Children or loved ones may teach you a lesson in self-discipline. Face life frankly and without complexes.

August—A Number Six Personal Year

This month is busy and in many ways exciting because of the freedom or different things brought about through the work and application of last month. You will be excited, pleased, and mentally more free, even though duty is still present. There is much to keep you busy and on the job. The month is progressive, and it is possible that you will be interested in or concerned with public affairs. Legal matters may come up to be taken care of, and it is well to see that all the practical undertakings of your personal and business interests are in proper legal form and order. There will be people coming and going, and you may be traveling or going places, too. In some way your ideas may change about your plans in regard to an association. You may even find that you are criticized, and you may be forced to take it and stand for what you feel is right. However, remember that this year is not a personal year, it is a duty year and stands for humanity and the welfare of others. Even the small things you do must in some way benefit others and be for the good of all if you are to really reap the future good which this year has promised. Service is really its keynote. New ideas and more life and surprises touched with the unexpected. Move forward and keep a progressive spirit. Health matters must still be given some consideration.

September—A Number Six Personal Year

The realization of duty and responsibility will be strong this month, although some of the details should gradually begin to lift as the fall of the year approaches. You should be able to look around you and see what has been accomplished and be pleased about it, even though you have paid quite a price in effort and character. As you still have to make adjustments in home matters and in regard to others, the broader aspect of your success and future should show up as worthwhile, especially if you have been a good sport and put yourself into your undertakings with courage and willing determination. The demands made upon you by others inside and outside of the home have built character and stamina and brought out the love and generosity of your nature. If you look back on the activities of the year and feel resentment and have hard feelings toward others, then you have not gained all the year offered you. And for a while, during this month, you will still have many demands upon your time, love, and pocketbook, but your general affairs are shaping into more settled arrangements certainly, clearing the way for more time for yourself and less duty during the coming year. Even though you will be doing many things for others, do not be discouraged. Health matters still demand attention and care. You may not like what others are doing, but if problems are talked over heart to heart and with mutual understanding and sympathy, they can be worked out satisfactorily. Love affairs, marriages, divorces, and all manner of human problems may touch your life this month, and probably have all during the year, giving you the chance to give wise counsel and to bring justice to the situations which come up. Be loving and give some of the love to others which in your heart, you seek for yourself. Love should color your dreams; love of home, family, work, children, and humanity gets the best results all year.

October—A Number Six Personal Year

You may find you are more alone in some respects this month than for some time. This can be of your own choosing and due to circumstances over which you have little control. You are likely to be mentally weary after the many, many tasks of the year and will need time to rest, relax, and be still, to read, study, and look at life from its deeper side. Even though you have many things settled and plans worked out, you will have a number of details to think out regarding the arrangements and methods by which you can lift some of the duty you have been carrying and still carry. There will be something you do not talk about or do not want people to know, and it is well to say very little, but be sure you keep a happy mental attitude even though there is some uncertainty present. This will work out all right if you keep an inner poise and faith and are willing to accept help. If you think that things are not as good as before, this may be just your own state of mind. This is a rest period, a sabbatical month, and it is best to watch, wait, and give time a chance. What you think you do not have will show up to help you next month if you do not disturb the progress of your life by worry and anxiety. Your business and home affairs will be adjusted regardless. Enjoy what you have accomplished this year. Diet and build up your nervous system, and do not be too serious in your approach to life and in regard to public affairs.

November—A Number Six Personal Year

Business activity this month, and it is a more public and progressive month than last. The poise gained and the faith maintained last month will support this month. Business activity should be carrying on and money should be managed or be gained through service and the influence you have gained during the year. Houses and property are to be considered, and some plan of reorganization may be born for final arrangements and improvements connected with the year's activities and adjustments. Be businesslike, for the way is there and there is no need to be overly anxious about results, if you are capable and clever. Gain harmony in all relationships and join with those who are successful in the world, for this will bring you assistance and give you some importance. In fact, the end of this year of service and responsibility should give you prominence or importance through the good work you have done with payments and settlement of business affairs and rewards you may not have counted on before.

December—A Number Six Personal Year

The last month of the year carries a very high force. It brings settlements, completions, and something pleasing in the way the year has turned out. You should be much happier concerning home and family matters, and find you can do much for those you love and those who have helped you. You do not need to carry too much Christmas responsibility, but you will feel happy to do for others and may find you are the one entertaining and still giving the service and inspiration. Christmas time is peculiar in some respects, even though you are happy, for you may be alone or away or conditions may not be as they usually are. There could be a slight disappointment in this and you might even feel left out of things, but on the whole you should find yourself receiving much love and appreciation. You may wonder in a way what to do next, now that so much has been accomplished and settled. Life will gradually turn your thoughts and talents in a new direction, for next year is your sabbatical year, and you will be interested in far different things. It may be February before this is realized. Right now you should have a foundation upon which to stand and only need time to open the door to new personal interests and opportunities.

Number

7

Right Action

Your Personal Year Guidance

From January 1st to December 31st

NUMBER SEVEN PERSONAL YEAR
RIGHT ACTION

General Trend

DOWN THROUGH THE ages the number seven has been associated with the occult, spiritual and mystical. However, it is often called the "lucky seven" in relationship to material interests and activities, symbolizing the "unexpected." As you make this year's progress toward your future success, you are likely to touch or even include all these interests, in various ways, for development of character, better understanding of yourself, your emotions and spiritual nature. You may wonder about this. You may even be disinclined to consider so-called religious interests as a necessary part of your work, success or business affairs, but after all, each personal year of every nine-year cycle is a step toward a better understanding of yourself, your ultimate goal in life; therefore, Right Action at the right time is a very important asset.

The Bible tells us that when the world was created, the Lord worked with concentration and energy for six days. Then He went away and rested. You are likely to feel an inner desire to be done with a lot of the work you carried on last year and the endless responsibility. The inner drive which will be prodding you now, will urge you to change your way of thinking and feeling and to live on a higher plane of thought and action. Regardless of your type of work, you may suddenly feel tired of the endless duties of last year, wish to have more time for yourself and be free from so many responsibilities, even from people and friends. This is a good year to take time out to rest, study, read, travel and to place some of the duties in the hands of others. Your Right Action now is not to be duty bound. The qualities of the soul are calling for creative expression and outlet. If you respond to this urge to know about your inner self and to think about beauty, perfection and what life is all about, over and above "getting on in the world," you will find the year a wonderful one with added rewards, not expected, to give you a realization of your rightful place in the world. Even in the midst of many things to do in your personal affairs, the key-note of the year is to gain understanding of spiritual laws for yourself and for a happier attitude of mind, at least.

You may find that you are more alone than usual. This is not misunderstanding, it is instead your opportunity to listen to the voice of your inner nature, telling you the truth about yourself, your character and your ability. Gather strength through rest and quiet times, even while you work. January through December this year, will be different than any other year in your present nine-year cycle. If you live it well and try to understand your experiences, you will be a changed person; looking at life from a different angle, with more confidence in yourself, your ability, your place in the world of endeavor, and your spiritual right to all that is good and worth-while being born for. The way you meet the experiences that are different will determine the trend of events as the year passes by. You are in the school of life this year and you should enjoy learning more about it and its deeper meaning. It is just as well to say little about it to others. Let the unfoldment come naturally and show in the way you begin to live your daily experiences.

Comment

You will find this a busy year, even though it is called a Sabbatical year. However, by February, many of your duties will be taken care of by others, or be completed due to your plans and desire for more time for yourself. From then on, the subtle force of the Number Seven will be employing or directing your attention toward new ways of thinking and acting through the experiences you are meeting, day by day. It may seem to you that you never have a moment to yourself, but at the same time, you will realize you are strangely more alone and that others seem to go their way, socially and otherwise. Also, you may unconsciously withdraw from their interests, even causing misunderstandings, in your mind as well as that of others. You may not be aware of this at first, but as the months pass by, you will enjoy the changes in your thought and feeling and be a better person. You will understand and realize that life is not just ''bread and butter,'' but a spiritual experience, natural, revealing and directing, as you go about your daily affairs.

One of the experiences you will need to prepare for, is that friends and loved ones may condemn you for your sudden interests in different ways of thinking and living. They may feel you are not like yourself, or they may argue with you about principles of thought and your new ways of thinking and feeling. It is just as well not to say much or to try to convince them. This may be about past interests and activities and ideals; separations and breaking up of friendships could result.

Changes in habits and interests often occur in a Seven Personal Year and stand for growth and progress. Work out all controversy in a quiet manner. The less said may be the better way and the Right Action all year long. By being poised and viewing life from a new angle, you will find the solution to all your problems. In this way, the "luck" of the year can come to you. Be glad you are you, for the year really places you in a position of strength, due to your inner poise and real effort to understand life better. You are the "thinker." When emotion and hurt feelings rule, problems will be aggravated and hard to solve.

Love affairs may enter in, having to do with the past, and be very rewarding. Take care of your health all year long. Get enough rest, and avoid haste. Enjoy being alone from time to time. Think, read, write, study, travel for educational reasons or interests. Join groups, both philosophical and educational. Meet new people and contribute something worthwhile to the progress of mankind.

Your Right Action colors for the year are: purple, brick, pearl, magenta and amethyst.

In business—attract and specialize
In marriage—try to understand each other
Children—teach silence and how to be alone
In-laws—do not argue
Human relationships—education is vital

MONTHS

Direct your understanding by the suggestions given for the months. Many of the following indications will take place, depending upon your character and the destiny you are born for, shown by your name at birth.

January—A Number Seven Personal Year

During this first month of the year, you will be busy with loose ends, and there will be many plans to think out and work with. Affairs having to do with property, possessions, and business arrangements are of the most importance and need to be managed and directed for release from some of the duty of the past months. It may take a few weeks more before you will clear away the duty and responsibility of last year, and right now you should be efficient and businesslike and do what you know is actually necessary to get results. There will be much expense connected with this or demands for money because of past obligations, and a decision will have to be made before the month is over, so it is advisable to estimate and appraise your ability and assets with good judgment and without too much personal feeling or sentiment. Others will still be involved, and it is very likely that you will be called upon to plan and manage for others as well as for yourself, but you should begin to see the way and to realize that your life is to be different from that of the past year. This will be based upon the fact that much of the past duty is behind you, that you are a little tired and want a change, and that new opportunity is present. The opportunity may not be exactly new but can be a channel or avenue through which you receive help or ideas to enable you to make the arrangements you have in mind. If you do not worry, the money of finances will be worked out all right, and enough money will be at hand to work out your plans.

February—A Number Seven Personal Year

This is one of the important months of the year because it brings so many things to a head. This may not be so apparent outwardly, for right now what you are thinking, and what you want for yourself, will influence your actions, and you should make an effort to think clearly and not allow yourself to be mentally confused or out of sorts. This is a sabbatical year, and some of your tasks, relationships, and duties must change or even be finished, through your own actions and through outside conditions, for only in this way can you eventually find the time to be more alone to read, study, or take up new mental or spiritual interests. So if you find you are more alone now and from now on, or that something is finished and you have little to do with what others are doing, do not mind or consider it a problem or annoyance. Just be glad that so much has been accomplished and that past duties have been completed. This month is a good time too, to be done with conditions or activities which you no longer feel are of importance to you, and you may honestly leave behind you or let go of some situation, if you do so graciously and without mis-understandings or arguments. The influence of this month is for endings, but the trend is for warmth of feeling, tolerance, and compassion, even though you are withdrawing your interest or activity. This month can be a very interesting and refreshing one if you keep big in spirit and *refuse* any·feeling of intol-erance or resentment. In this way there will be a pleasing reward, and the law of "attraction" will begin to operate, bringing you help, unexpected good, and personal satisfaction. This month carries the prophecy of the changes, separations, and the new setup which your sabbatical year naturally brings to you.

March—A Number Seven Personal Year

Last month was not a good time to push any matter in a forceful or willful manner, for there was so much to think out. However, during March you will find more opportunity to take action upon the plans and conclusions of last month relative to the future. In fact, you can now go ahead with new plans, and should be looking forward and not back. The future is the important thing. Of course, this is only the third month of the year, and there are many experiences ahead. Full results are not likely to be gained right away, but you can go ahead quietly and determinedly now and begin to get plans in order. Do not be too forceful or self-interested, for even though this is your year to be on your own, your interests should not be selfish or too self-centered, for you should, by now, have gained a great deal of experience and wisdom, and should be able to understand yourself and how to get on with others. Misunderstanding, the little fox in the vines this year, is hanging around and could begin to destroy harmony, should you be unkind. If others impose upon you, make your position or ideas about things very clear with courage and dignity, but do not become involved in the domestic and business problems of others more than you feel is right. If you meet delay or opposition, remember that your secret for getting results this year is through deep inner poise and faith and not force or dominance directed toward others or outside conditions. Enjoy being busy and doing different things. Get a lot of rest, too, for health's sake.

April—A Number Seven Personal Year

Even though this is a sabbatical year and should give you time to be more alone and on your own, it will be a busy year in many ways. Right now, during April, you will be aware of this and find yourself doing many things, a good many of which are not too important. You should begin to realize this now and do everything with patience and cooperation, and it will be better in the end if you take the time to get these jobs done and to work out the details tactfully with others. In the matters which are important to you, be sure that you know what you are doing and why. Look underneath the surface, for outwardly you may not see the right direction to go. Perhaps, a little more time is needed. There are details to attend to in getting ready for the personal plans which you have in mind for May. This is a good time to take up a study and to begin mental or spiritual training. The love affairs of others and also your own emotional problems may take on new color and interest and give you something to think about. You could meet people who are different and prove interesting and helpful, although these contacts may not be permanent or lasting. All during this month keep moods and dispositions under control and refuse to be hard to understand because of the way you are thinking or acting now. It seems a good thing to say very little about what you are working toward until the end of this month or until next month opens up. Look after your health and give your glands and nervous system a boost, for this will help you keep well and get more enjoyment out of the many tasks you have to do.

May—A Number Seven Personal Year

You should be conscious of a happier state of mind all during this spring month because so many little things have been worked out, and also because you managed so well last month through the patience and tact you used to swing things into line with your desires. This is a fine time to take a vacation or a trip, or even if you have planned a trip for July, which is a very good time for change and freedom, you should do something for the sake of fun or pleasure during May. Follow the inspiration or impulse to do creative work, to study, write, read, or to give expression to your artistic or religious feelings or to your talents. Especially, find an outlet for the ideas of personal nature which have been going around in your mind and heart for a long time. Make this a constructive effort and something worthwhile; otherwise if you live in moods or hurt feelings and talk out of turn, you will regret it very much, and the rest of the year may bring an inner sorrow or regret. There are likely to be emotional upsets because of others, and you will feel very deeply about what is happening to friends, relatives, or loved ones, but it is not likely that you can do much about it but be kind, helpful, and understanding. In many ways, this is one of the turning points of the year, and you should think and understand your own feelings and use wisdom and discretion in dealing with others. Walk serenely on to victory over self and the disturbing situations with dignity, self-control, faith, and inner poise. Get a bit of fun out of this month and be a good friend.

June—A Number Seven Personal Year

The tone of this month is different from that of last month, for again you seem to be called upon to get down to work and to be practical. At least, you need to deal with the ideas of last month in a practical way to place the foundation for the projects and interests of next month. You may feel serious and uninspired or even let down, but you should snap out of this for there is work to be done, order to be gained, and much to be managed to get things ready for future activity. You must manage and see that everything is running smoothly. Even if you feel some economic pressure, do not make this a problem, for you will be able to manage in the end. This is not a good time to take a vacation or to promote interests. As you are very practical, work with the things at hand, and get your affairs in better order. There could be papers to sign and contracts to consider, and you are likely to feel that matters are too slow, but you cannot hurry anything. Even if you seem to be the burden bearer, say nothing, and dig in to whatever has to be done. Look after your health this month, for you could experience digestive upsets or feel a lack of energy. Just keep your feet on the ground for the time being, and do what is necessary to get the results you anticipate. Do not shirk, but on the other hand, do not work too hard. There is a medium ground which is found through inner patience, poise, and the sense of your inner power. The same misunderstanding could crop up again this month, but you can manage it and not be hurt by it if you analyze conditions wisely and remember that this is not your duty year. If you have not gained understanding of situations and are still bothered by them, get the advice of an understanding person, friend, or lawyer. Conditions are temporary, and you will feel differently next month.

July—A Number Seven Personal Year

A deeper sense of freedom should be experienced this month, and you should take a trip, go places, and do things. If this seems impossible, at least find some new interest—a study, a book, lecture, or sport which will bring variety and renewed interest. The month will be eventful of its own accord and will bring new interests, new contacts, new people into your affairs. In many ways, you will be doing different things because of the practical management and work of last month. You may feel restless and discontented at times, and you can make changes and be done with responsibilities which have bothered you. There is a helpful influence in the month, and if you keep alert and active and are resourceful, the affairs of life and those about you will bring interest and varied experience. You should be doing a lot of thinking and self-analysis during these summer months. A strong desire for new life and better expression of your talents should be in the back of your mind. July is a good time to take steps to improve your mind, to reach out for mental food, and for contact with or interest in the mental and intellectual activities of the world. You can have a good time, too, but do not be hasty or hurried, and avoid risks or any undertaking which is done hastily or with impulse, as your sabbatical year demands character and dignity, pride and wisdom, and intelligent action all year through. Take good care of legal matters and keep up-to-date in everything you do. Even though your sabbatical year keeps you a little in the background, it does not keep you out of progressive activity or undertakings.

August—A Number Seven Personal Year

You may be surprised to find yourself in the midst of responsibility this month and be wondering where the aloneness of the year has gone. Family matters, duty, and adjustments due to affairs of the home and relatives are likely to appear, but this may be pleasant, too, and of your own making, especially if you have taken a trip or are visiting. This duty should be interesting and pleasant, but will keep you very busy, and you may find something of a pleasing nature through children or younger people. The duty is only for this month, so take it nicely, express a lot of sympathy for others, and help them with their problems. A restriction or a limitation may be present, but you should not mind this, for through talking things over and doing what must be done, you can adjust matters, and in the end have a better idea of what is being left behind and the interesting changes which the year has promised. It may seem for a time that there are interruptions to your plans, and this could be slightly depressing, but this is just to help you understand conditions, yourself, and to look your plans over again to make sure you have them well arranged and thought out. If you do not seem to move forward at all, just go back to your studies, your reading, and the quiet care of your health. Even if you feel really well, take time out now and then for complete relaxation and simple pleasures, for in your next Personal Year you must take up business affairs and get back your ambition.

September—A Number Seven Personal Year

There is an element of surprise or luck this month. This may come through others or work you have accomplished in past months and even past years. The *law of attraction* is working for you now and is the best method you can use to get things done during September. The mental work you have done during the spring and summer should begin to bring results, in the way of self-control and also through quiet work and study. It is necessary for you to keep a poised control of conditions and of yourself, for it may seem to you now and then, that others are wrong, that you are wrongly placed or in the wrong environment. You can change this to a degree through patient endeavor, but it may be just as well not to strive for anything and let things take their course. Take a trip for rest or change, keep your health up to par, and work for inner peace and faith. Others may not live up to their agreements and be rather trying. You will discover something about yourself or others which will help you make later plans, and it is very likely to be apparent to you that a sort of crisis is beginning to shape up coming to a head in November. If you feel you are alone or not treated right, just mind your own affairs and let others take care of theirs, not selfishly but wisely, and save a lot of unnecessary talk or even arguments. Keep your mind and heart happy, your body rested, and be ready for the next activity. Something will be revealed or you will get a hunch about what to do, and this will open the way for more business activity next month. Watch and wait and keep constructively busy.

October—A Number Seven Personal Year

After the quiet endeavor of last month, this month will seem a very busy one. Business affairs come up for consideration and rearrangement, and there will be matters of buying and selling, organization and reorganization to take care of. Papers and property matters call for attention and good judgment, and a lot of running back and forth and coming and going will be connected with your work and home affairs. Many other people will be involved and a good many things seem to be in the process of preparation, and this is likely to be about finals and endings which are more definite and certain with November. You may now begin to sense the business goal of next year and may be eager to be up and doing. There is a bridge to cross before this can take place, and you should look far ahead now. Actually give your time to taking care of the things at hand which call for business attention and management. Someone about you may be hard to deal with or seem to turn on you or be unreasonable, but this is not of too much importance, especially if you remember not to say too much, even now that the year is almost over. A new angle or viewpoint about business and things in general will be gained by the time this month is over and November is under way. A business offer and a chance to get rid of some old conditions is a likely experience during October.

November—A Number Seven Personal Year

A good many of the experiences, plans, and activities of the year have been leading toward the finals and endings which are part of November. Life may take a hand and direct your affairs toward these finals, but on the other hand, the closing experiences may consist only of your own deep conclusions and decision to be done with matters which do not bring you personal happiness or progress. If you have had the courage to stand on your own feet and to be yourself, even though you have not said much about it to others, you should find that circumstances and also friends and loved ones will help you take the steps you desire and assist you in bringing about final arrangements for future progress. On the other hand, you may have to give up something or stand aside, while others work out their future also. In many respects, this can be a little confusing, but if you will just try to realize that life is always on the march and moving forward, and are willing to move forward yourself, even if the way is not all clear or you are not absolutely sure of the future, you will find many rewards and many blessings running through the activities which now and then may seem to be out from under your control. It is probable that some of this is not really your problem, that you are only looking on, but it will affect you and could mean the end of an association or interest and a marked change in your life. Out of it all should come a deep soul development, for a sabbatical year is not a material year, and it is what you think and how much soul and character development you make during this year that really counts, whether you are interested in doing so or not. Summing up: many things in your life will be adjusted during November to go on at a new level and in an interesting way. Be generous in feeling, compassionate, and forgiving in your approach to others, and contemplate the higher ideals and meanings. This is really a command from life itself.

December—A Number Seven Personal Year

The influence of the sabbatical year now begins to pass. You can plan to take advantage of the business opportunities which are present or in your mind. Pick them up and sort them out for worth, future progress and use, as your business year approaches. However, there is a short period of finals and tasks to be taken care of in *January* of next year, so what you do now is in the nature of rearrangements, rather than to force any issue. Remember this! It may be *February* of next year before you can move forward with full direction and opportunity. This is likely to be due to happenings or a few delays you had not counted on. This Christmas month will be busy, and different in some respect. Look for a trip, visitors, the unexpected, but with more freedom and new interests. The subtle force which was operating all year to help you understand yourself, is now passing and from now on you will need to stand on your own feet, use good business judgment, and put your energies to work to produce tangible results. Make this a pleasant Christmas and gather your mental judgment and energies together for a forward effort next year.

Number

8

Right Action

Your Personal Year Guidance

From January 1st to December 31st

NUMBER EIGHT PERSONAL YEAR
RIGHT ACTION

General Trend

YOUR RIGHT ACTION this year is "achievement." It is up to you to put forth the effort to gain the results you dream of or are capable of attaining. It is your underlying motive in all you do, all year long. It is the next to last year of your present nine-year cycle of experience and growth and the right time to present your talents for recognition and reward.

It is like harvest time to the farmer, when his produce is brought to market. You need to be ready now to move forward in a businesslike manner with efficiency, resourcefulness and sustained effort to gain the reward, and to hold on to the benefits the year promises. Whatever your employment or means of earning a living—doctor, lawyer, merchant, artist, entertainer, writer, salesman, craftsman, inventor, minister, or if you are daily employed by others, make a special effort to improve and bring to a successful conclusion, some of the ideas and dreams of the past years of the cycle's tests, trials, successes, even failures, as the year passes by.

Many opportunities will present themselves, during the year. You will need to seek out these opportunities for yourself. Your state of mind, your mental capacities and self-confidence will all be a part of your success and financial advancement. In other words, nothing will be gained by just "hoping." This is a year of action. Whatever your ability, place it on the market with a sense of self-confidence and authority. Then be ready to back up your effort by hard work and skill in dealing with business ways and means by which success is attained. It is, after all, not the money to be made *that really matters,* it is your strength of character, stamina and sustained ambition all year long.

The symbol of the year is like the "Horn of Plenty," small at the beginning, but expanding into abundance and plenty; all depending upon your steady effort, good judgment concerning your future and good every-day business common sense.

Join with those who are working for improvement in your line of endeavor or talents. Do not work entirely alone. Get advice from those in authority or capable of helping you. Brains seem to count this year. Not much will be gained by emotional out-breaks or by scattering your forces or lack of personal discipline, when trying for results.

Think! Make your efforts worthwhile; for others as well as yourself.

Comment

All these requirements indicate this is not to be an easy year. Financial matters will call for attention and are likely to force you to organize or reorganize your personal affairs as well as business undertakings. It is important that you do not overestimate your ability, early in the year; take the time to know what you want to do. Face all issues with a keen mind and renewed ambition. Stress or worry over money may delay your success and make the year harder than it should be.

There will be many interesting happenings as part of the year's experiences, even the possibility of trips, long or short, combining business, pleasure, and social activity.

Love affairs may prove stimulating, and the meeting of interesting people may add to the interest and progress of the year. However, choose your associates wisely. This is a year to advance your standing and position in the world; it could be a waste of time to be indiscreet or careless where morals are concerned, in business or personal interests. Recognize your own way of life and standard of living as this year brings its challenge.

Health matters run through the year. Take good care of your digestive system and do not allow strain or over-intensity of feeling about anything to get you down. Take time out to rest and to let down now and then, especially when it seems hard to make ends meet.

Family matters will call for attention. Do not be dominant, but help others to find the way to work out their own problems as you are working out your own.

As the year ends, you should be well established in work and environment. Gradually you will realize that you have done all that you can do for now, and experience the feeling that you are finished with a work, or old condition although deeply attached to the old relationship. Do not pass judgment. Keep a warm heart even in the midst of business and many demands upon your time and judgment.

Find a cause or purpose to work for, for the betterment of mankind—political, worldly or spiritually. An interest or plan, having meaning for all mankind, will call for your thought and endeavor.

Your Right Action colors are: canary, buff, tan, opal, ivory and turquoise.

> In business—seek and give counsel
> In marriage—do not be dominant
> Children—teach money and banking values
> In-laws—encourage self-reliance
> Human relationships—interest in the good of mankind in a philosophical pattern.

MONTHS

Much of the following will take place; at least there is a tendency for it to happen or work out, depending on your character and the forces at work shown by your name at birth. People differ in their responses to life's pressures and individual destiny. Pick out the good and directional advice given for each personal year and month, and keep a firm control over your affairs to prevent the possibility of the negative trend getting the upper hand. Following the advice for the year and the month will help you have confidence in what you are doing for the best results and personal advancement.

January—A Number Eight Personal Year

During this month, there will be something to decide about your property or your possessions. This is a rather strong decision and may be about a house or living quarters. The decision may be connected with a plan to get rid of something in order to arrange for new ideas or interests. For a while, you may feel uncertain or confused, but gradually your mind will begin to clear in regard to last year's affairs and there will be opportunity present to get ready for the new and the future. This decision may be simply a reorganization of your activities for better order and system both at home and in business, and will be based upon ambition and a desire to be up and doing. Keep your goal in mind, even though circumstances may delay you for the time being. There may be a disappointment in something, but this is probably because a little more time was needed or because you were in too much of a hurry and did not look far enough ahead. Legal affairs may enter into the month, and you may leave something behind, to clear the way for more definite action next month. Color your motives, activities, and feelings with compassion, tolerance, and forgiveness this month, even in this business year. This is *not the time* to ask favors, or force issues; instead, attend to what is at hand.

February—A Number Eight Personal Year

This is one of the important months of the year, for now is a time to take action and to go ahead with your plans connected with business and family matters, and especially along lines which give you more self-expression. There is much to think about now, and it is possible that family matters or some member of the family may be a problem, but you will find the trend favorable for moving forward along almost all the lines or plans you have in mind. The trend of events will begin to show itself and you should feel pleasure or inspiration in this. Take problems in your stride, keep a firm hold on things, and take the initiative, for this is a "beginning time" and a time to go ahead. Results may not be fully apparent, and it is just as well to talk things over with others. Unless everything is faced frankly now, there could be frustrations rather than progress. You can win your point if you really have a good plan, are using good judgment, and have appraised your ability. You are half-way between the old and the new and the new is opening up nicely now. The things you have started can roll along and give a feeling of advancement even though there are a few hindrances mixed in. It is possible that you may receive an offer or proposal which will please you, and you can make money or obtain the help you need to help you push things forward.

March—A Number Eight Personal Year

You should begin to experience a lot of satisfaction now because of the results you are beginning to get and because a lot of little things do not seem to matter any more. This should give you a happier state of mind. You should now be able to do what you have wanted to do and have been planning for some time and in association with others. You do need help and intelligent advice now for some sort of organization in your plans. In fact, all during this busy year you have others to consider and work with, to get the best results.

You will be challenged by the opinions of associates, but new conditions will interest you and new ways and means open up. This is a social month, and is a good time to mix with others, and to express the graciousness and courtesy which are due those you are in association with or meet in your daily affairs.

Here is where your good disposition is an asset, to make sure the rest of the year is happy and that you do not have to worry because you did not put your best foot forward. Some little thing of a *personal nature* can be very annoying to you because you cannot change it right away. Show patience, for some of the activities taking place this month are temporary or only stepping stones to more freedom for you personally. Keep your goal in mind in spite of a few delays.

April—A Number Eight Personal Year

Last month should have shown you the general trend of affairs and the way your plans are going to set up for a while. This month is important, for the bigger results which the year promises should be in the air or be giving you inspiration and courage. This month gives you the chance to follow your personal desires and to do things for yourself, especially along the lines of art, music, inspiration, and activities in which your heart and deeper nature are interested. But remember that this year is not a time for impulse or foolish action. You need to exercise good judgment and efficiency and to again estimate your ability and opportunity to get immediate results. In this way, you will save yourself mental strain and anxiety, especially so if you look well ahead and are satisfied to get results step by step.

There is nothing wrong about this; it is simply to get you to look into details and get a true perspective. Do not sign away future rights in any arrangement just to get temporary results right now. There is much at stake, and you need to stand for your rights but continue to add inspiration and creative imagination to your work and to the plans you are undertaking.

Have the courage to take a step in a new direction if you feel the need, but manage both the present and the future, for they are together now. There should be pleasure, entertainment, and maybe a trip as the result of this month's activities, and you are likely to spend some money. Do not be extravagant, but do something to add color and inspiration to your daily undertakings. A good month to write letters, attend lectures and activities which represent culture and the finer things of life.

May—A Number Eight Personal Year

This is a very practical month and may seem hard after the inspiration of last month. You may even feel discouraged or not up to par. Take care of your health and do not eat too much. Face facts, no matter what they are. It is necessary to get results now, and there is work connected with this. A good many things must be managed and put in their places. In order to get concrete results now, which the month demands, you will find an exact need for organizing or reorganizing matters. Your ability to work hard and to understand practical values must be brought to bear upon all activities. There can be annoyance about money at first, but in the end, you can manage all right if you keep your head and do not allow yourself to be confused by others or the demands of others in the present situation. Think your way through and be sure you know what you are doing, especially if you are called upon to sign papers or contracts. In many ways, you may not like this month, but the details, the slower tempo, and the practical matters are important because the foundation which must be worked out during the year is now beginning to take on more definite form. Ask advice of those who know. You will receive help in this way if you ask for it and face facts. Keep plugging along and follow through to the end of all plans or undertakings. The requirements of your family may call for care or attention, too, and there could be illness to consider in family matters. If you put your shoulder to the wheel, you will see things through. This all sounds terrific, but in fact, it is only the present need to get things done that brings the work and responsibility to fulfillment.

June—A Number Eight Personal Year

This month will be a relief after the serious feeling of May. You will experience a sense of freedom and more excitement due to the changes brought about by the practical endeavor of last month. June will bring a great deal of activity and new interests or new contacts. It is possible that you may travel, be moving about, or at least be doing something different for the time being and be enjoying it greatly. There is the possibility of a few annoyances in the month to be taken care of, however, and your own disposition again needs to be under control to make sure you do not say things hastily or impulsively which may cause annoyance or a problem between you and someone else. Put your best foot forward all month and be alert and resourceful in meeting people or the public, for there is something for you to gain through association or contact with many people. Legal matters and property interests bring details to take care of. There is a possibility that there will be some change in what has been planned, but there is much to be gained, too, through an association or partnership during this month. The trend of the month is for new ideas through helping others, while at the same time you reach out for new interests for your own good. A trip this month or next on business and pleasure, even if it is of short duration, is in order.

July—A Number Eight Personal Year

A great deal of responsibility appears this month due to family affairs and the changes and excitement of last month. There are adjustments to be made regarding others or with others, and there is something to figure out for yourself. You will be more clear in mind and get better results if you talk things over, kindly and helpfully, and for the good of all concerned. Illness may bring a care or expense. Doctors, nurses, or hospitals may be a part of the month's experiences. Children or young people may bring interest and care and also require your patience and sympathy. A number of things can be loaded on your shoulders during the month; and you seem to be compelled to meet the responsibility, but even so you do not need to give up your plans for personal and business progress. You can get a lot of pleasure out of your activities during July, even though you do have much to do, if you will just keep cheerful. Money affairs can be adjusted for general benefit, even though they are slow. Love affairs may interest you or at least friendship should bring you admiration and a touch of romance.

August—A Number Eight Personal Year

This month is a quiet one and would be a good time to take a vacation if you can, not so much for a good time as for rest and relaxation. You have done a lot up to now, and there will be a deep realization of what you have done, planned, and undertaken (perhaps on your own) to rearrange and organize your affairs during the past months. You may think results are not right, but they are all right underneath the surface, and at present there is not much you can do about them. You may feel alone, but if you say very little and do not allow yourself to worry, everything will work out all right of its own accord. The truth is that the struggle is going on in your own mind and heart, more than is on the outside, and you need time to rest and think and to get hold of your thoughts and feelings. This is best done by getting away for awhile if you can. You might feel in the doghouse, but at the same time will be getting pleasure out of your actions and the task or work you have accomplished up to the present time. Business difficulties can straighten themselves out nicely, and you will find that you are in control of your affairs more than you had at first thought possible when the month began. You will be doing a lot of thinking about yourself and your rights and personal freedom, and should begin to get the hunch that you want to make further changes or improvements. This will be based on the right to do and dare and to be yourself. In thinking this out, look well to the future and far back into the past, and do not be personal, selfish, or sentimental. What you do this fall and from now on must be based upon good business ability and good judgment and not entirely upon likes and dislikes. Take up a new study this month, and do a few things which make you happy in a personal manner and in an intellectual way. Diet, too, for health's sake. Keep your poise and have little to say about what others do. Faith and poise are the month's keynotes.

September—A Number Eight Personal Year

You should begin to feel now as though you are getting circumstances under control again, and realize that you have truly accomplished a business and financial improvement and general advancement through your mental and practical efforts, in spite of the mental strain you have felt from time to time. This year has been a big year and has laid the foundation for the future in more ways than you can realize at present. It has been more than a business year demanding your best in the way of business effort and also your best in the way of character.

A determination is present to be free from something which has not made you happy and has made it hard for you or tried to destroy your peace of mind. It is the influence of the spiritual part of the year. Try to get free mentally, that is, in your own mind, by not caring so much and by not allowing little things to matter. If you cannot attain this inner freedom, then have the courage to be done with the old, for peace of mind is more than money and a tranquil attitude of mind and thought will smooth out both financial and emotional difficulties. Do not act in a headstrong way; get advice and counsel from those in power and authority in order to know what you should do and to help you keep from making a mistake as you weigh the past and the future. Love affairs seem to have a lot to do with the decisions and the inner unrest you may be feeling, and it is advisable not to turn away from true love or tried friendship for the sake of money or possessions. A feeling that you do not care or are no longer interested may be beginning to enter your mind. Do not let this be mixed with resentment. Instead, realize you are gaining wisdom; and have learned to know the worth of right action over and above your personal feelings. New ideas color the old activity and help you let go of circumstances not worthwhile. It may take all the rest of the year, and perhaps into next spring before you fully complete the activities and conditions which now fill your mind and heart with determination.

October—A Number Eight Personal Year

A good many activities come to a head now, and it would be well if any misunderstandings between yourself and others were straightened out in a sensible manner, otherwise someone or something may go out of your life which could bring regret later. You should be certain in your own mind as to what you want to do about your own progress and activities and go ahead with them, but you need to be very sure, otherwise someone may be hurt and your actions may look bad to them. In some way, you will realize that you are at the end of an activity or plan, and as you move forward into next month's activity, look well under the surface to the details of your undertakings and know just where you stand. There is a demand for love, tolerance, and compassion, and this may be one of the times when it is well not to be too proud, and to swallow your pride, unless you are very sure you want to go ahead with the final arrangements. This is a good time to be done with any possession or circumstance that has outlived its usefulness, or with anything which keeps you from moving forward in an enterprising and worthwhile way. Give thought to religion and to philosophical teaching. This will help you get on the right track. The love affairs of others may be thrust upon you, but not for long. Do not get too involved, but be helpful. These changes are not necessarily momentous, mostly conclusions, mentally and philosophically, to help you plan your own way of life.

November—A Number Eight Personal Year

This will prove to be a very busy month, as many things will happen due to outside conditions and to what you have planned, influenced by the coming and going of others and *their* plans. Much will be revealed all of a sudden, to help you take the step in regard to property, business, and love affairs which you know to be necessary. Your courage will be strengthened by the finals which take place; and a new light can be thrown upon your interests and activities. Give yourself the ''once over'' for health's sake and take care of illness around you, for it may be more serious than it seems on the surface. You may not be sure of every step for the next two or three months, but it is better to move forward than to stand still, especially in the direction of self-improvement as well as that of business. You should be conscious of a new work or a new way of thinking, and find much interest and inspiration in this. A month of beginnings and endings.

December—A Number Eight Personal Year

This closing month of the year is an important one as it is a period of transition. There seem to be two ways to go. If you have been true to yourself and have lived up to your best character without pride or feelings of discouragement as the experiences have come up to test your ability and business efficiency, the way will open up and show itself to you; and you will gain so much satisfaction from this that you will feel that it has all been worthwhile. If you have been careless or *fought* for your rights, and have thought of money and fine living more than good will, you may be conscious of a loss and not know just what you want to do, and experience a breaking up or a separation. But this may be good, too, and open a new field of endeavor and lead to a good many interesting and intriguing experiences. If you find something is breaking up and you do not want this to take place, then it is vitally important to be diplomatic, tactful, and to cooperate with others and circumstances. Prayer and spiritual thought will overcome discord or disharmony, defeating the negative condition or the loss and aloneness which might come otherwise. There is work and duty for you to assume, and you should be very interested in this. Someone will help you, and your own efforts should bring you the means to carry out your plans. You may feel a little tired after the work and endeavor of the year, so enjoy Christmas and take time for pleasant little things and happy social activities. Next month, in January, you enter upon the last year of your present cycle of experience. It will be a time to accept and receive, rather than to force issues. Your business ability, good judgment and positive direction of your affairs on all levels of living, is your Right Action all during your Number Eight Personal Year.

Number

9

Right Action

Your Personal Year Guidance

From January 1st to December 31st

NUMBER NINE PERSONAL YEAR
RIGHT ACTION

General Trend

T HIS YEAR BRINGS many of your affairs to a head. *Between January of this year and January of next year* you will realize a completion and also the fulfillment of some of your dreams. You are now closing a cycle of experience, one that you began nine years ago, leading to a beginning and a new start with next year. The completion is not a failure or sorrow. It is in reality a reward, for through it you open the way to new opportunities and new interests in life. During the year you must be ready and willing to let go of the old and undesirable in your life, to make way for the new and worthwhile. It is important to make a definite effort to be done with things which have no further value. If something you are trying to hold on to asks for freedom or desires to get away, be understanding, for if you try to hold it, it may get away anyway, especially if life sees fit to make this change. Be tolerant, compassionate, and forgiving, and then you will find this one of the most wonderful years of your life, for a reward of love, sympathy, understanding, and fulfillment of your plans may bring financial assistance as well as loving appreciation.

During the early winter and spring, affairs should improve and bring you an opportunity to do what you feel is necessary. During the summer you may feel alone, held back, and unable to keep things moving forward in a steady manner. Do not try to do so. Give life a chance to help you, and keep your mind open to broader interests and larger activities which can be born now, even though not carried out fully until the new cycle opens with next year. During the year you may find your interests growing away from some of your former associations and activities and unconsciously turn your thought and attention to interests which have not been a part of your life before. Make these interests of universal nature and avoid being small, personal, and selfish, for this could lead to disappointment in the end. Love affairs will hold your attention, others if not your own, and you may find you are involved in these without your desire. There is something for you to do to help others straighten out their affairs, for this is a year of impersonal thought and feeling and what you do for others will be rewarded.

This is *not* a good time to start new issues. The tide of life is out rather than in. Keep busy and accept opportunity if it comes to you, but until September you may not see the way clearly and will need to make changes and adjustments because of the closing force of the year. Do not overwork. Take a vacation in July. Your health must be kept up to par, for you have much to do next year. The fall of the year finds you marking time, going slowly, but with mutual assistance if you are cooperative and generous in your thought and feeling. If something goes out of your life, let it go, for it is clearing the way to your future happiness and good.

Comment

This closing year of your present nine-year cycle is a very interesting one. It is like the graduating year from college and tries to bring you the reward of your endeavors—in its own way. Under the nine influence, universal thought and feeling should be uppermost even though you are busy with personal interests. The "brotherhood of man" is the keynote with good will toward others. Number nine is the number of love which, impersonal and universal, belongs to all. It cannot be claimed for one's self alone. It belongs to the whole world. As the year passes, respond to the silent urge to do good works in order that humanity or the world in general will be happier. Do this without thought of personal gain or reward.

You too, this year, belong to those who promote civilization and work for the betterment of mankind. Even if you cannot consciously take part in such endeavor, let your heart be filled with compassion, tolerance, and forgiveness, even for your so-called enemies. The experiences of the year will tend to broaden and widen your own scope of activity. Whatever your talent, profession, or work, be a little bigger and kinder in your thoughts and aspirations.

During this year there will be finals, endings, conclusions, something to give up. It is a sort of clearinghouse period to give you a new outlook and a glimpse of the future, with less duty; time for relaxation and a sense of inner satisfaction.

While the year clears up many old problems, it also

tests your character. You may be called upon to give up a relationship, or leave something behind, even a way of living, whether you wish to or not. This is not a sacrifice; it is necessary so that you may go ahead with plans for your own broader expression. In the end this can be a great relief. Have the courage to let go, estimate the worth of what must be given up. It may have no further value to you. Some old situation will take care of itself if you allow it its freedom. You should feel a sense of power when the change is finally made because you will see the need for the adjustment for both yourself and others.

There will be a slight disappointment in regard to some of the details and some uncertainty about how everything will turn out, but this is of minor importance. The old could not go on because it no longer has a place in the work the future has in store for you.

Love affairs run through the year. Some of the problems of the year may be the result of deep emotional feeling regarding your relationship with loved ones, if not your own, that of others. Marriage can be a reward when the attraction has been of long duration, but in the same way, happiness may be the result of a companionship outlived. Your lesson may be to let go rather than to hold on when the attraction is over.

During the year you may often feel tired, not always equal to your work. Find time to rest and work out your emotions in some friendly way. Do not worry or try too hard to do more than you should. You have had many tasks and problems, but they are not entirely your responsibility. Let life and others shoulder some of them.

You may even feel a sense of frustration and futility from time to time, a sort of "what's the use" feeling. Refuse to have these moods, especially during the summer. Take a vacation, a quiet one, in July if you can, with an interesting companion. If you find yourself alone, realize that this is a time to give thought to spiritual development. Take up a study, travel, and enjoy cultural and creative activities. Money should be there all year, especially when you lend a hand to others.

During the last three months of the year, you will be marking time, as there is not much you can do for a while. Take care of your health and relax, and have the patience to wait. Enjoy everyday affairs, join with others in the spirit of companionship.

Your Right Action colors are: all colors.

In business—service for all people
In marriage—understanding gives love's mystic beauty
Children—teach compassion
In-laws—they are God's people too
Human relationships—philanthropy above charity

MONTHS

Direct your undertakings by the suggestions given for the month. Many of the following indications will

take place depending upon your character and the destiny you are born for, shown by your name at birth.

January—A Number Nine Personal Year

All during this month you will be doing a lot of thinking and will still be a little uncertain about the future. You are likely to have a desire for change and to be more settled. It may still take time to bring the fulfillment and the reward of the year. There are channels to be explored. There are many ends and threads to be taken up and tied together and some cut off to bring you the real freedom the year has for you. Keep all doubts and fears under control, for impulse or too much personal feeling could bring problems and offset the reward. Review your life during the past eight years and choose in your heart what you would like to keep. Know what you have learned and gradually new plans for living will begin to take form in your mind and heart. Be efficient, use executive ability, and do not neglect the things at hand. January may seem like a new beginning in some way in that you are living or acting in a different situation. You will be doing a lot of thinking and making plans regarding old conditions, although the new may be part of them. This month indicates the need of reorganization for a better basis of *understanding.* A new realization regarding associations and a lesson of tolerance and compassion will be learned because of the necessities of the moment. There will be a few fears and doubts but you can find this a very vital month, turning the old into new opportunity or new relationships.

February—A Number Nine Personal Year

You will be in the midst of a great deal of activity during this month. You will experience assistance through others, and beneficial ideas can be realized or given to you. This is more than objective assistance. It comes through inspirational ideas, so keep your mind open to higher things and to help that can come out of the blue. Keep your own faith in the good in life out on the surface. Many plans will move along slowly for the time being and you will be involved in the affairs of others, and must consider others to get what you want personally. Keep poised and cheerful. Be a little careful of what you say in too frank a manner, for there is an undercurrent of annoyance through what others do. You can be hurt quite unexpectedly. You may even find it hard to talk to those most concerned because you think something is unfair. Do not take this too seriously, for it may not be a very important thing, simply something which surprises and disturbs you emotionally. Consult someone outside the picture and get good advice. Do not try to work it out entirely by your own ideas. Patience and tact are needed qualities at this time. Say little until it passes or is explained. The month should show you some sign of the trend of events of the year. A social month and interesting things in the way of social entertainment. Make new friends. Try for beneficial associations. They are worthwhile this month and can help you. It is not likely you can manage or direct activities entirely on your own. There is a duty present. Keep poised. At the same time express diplomacy and willingness to share, to get the best results.

March—A Number Nine Personal Year

You should feel a little more free this month and find opportunity to do some of the things you want to do in a way you desire and without so much interference from others. An idea or new inspiration and help through friends should give a lift to your feelings. Social activities, parties, and the possibility of something pleasing, through admiration expressed to you. Old friends you have not seen for some time may give you inspiration. There is still the possibility of a slight annoyance through friends and relatives. Remember this is your year for tolerance and compassion at all times. You will be conscious of the desire to be done with an old association all during the year, and at the same time you are likely to be aware that an old condition has changed or is changing. Put your thoughts, at this time, into what you are doing, for others as well as for yourself. You have the right to be personal now, though not carelessly, for the future must be kept in mind or waited for. During March a new interest may come through a friend or a line of work or study which will give you the opportunity or pave the way for you to do something which gives new interest and inspiration in your own way. This seems to be a relief, almost like a vacation, so that some of the difficulties may fade away for the time being. Cultivate your interest in art and creative endeavor which can bring contacts in spite of some criticism by family or friends. Do not take this too seriously. Go ahead with what you think is right and good. You should realize an admiration for what you are and do. The love affairs of others may bring emotional experiences to be taken care of.

April—A Number Nine Personal Year

This month is a practical one and brings facts to the surface. You are apt to be forced to face economic conditions in a very definite manner. This could be due to business interests and to the fact that you know in your own mind you cannot go on in the old way. You will be faced with practical considerations and may consider a move or change of residence. Even though you may feel annoyed and slightly discouraged, there is an opportunity present to rearrange the business and emotional affairs which have needed adjustment for some time. Concentrate on getting results and be willing to do what is necessary even if results are not just what you had hoped for. Matters having to do with property, legal papers, and agreements call for the best possible management and good judgment. The work done now should form a basis for progress during the next few months. Some of this may concern the finals which your Number Nine Personal Year demands. This month may seem almost too practical and a little more demanding than you were prepared for. You may feel alone or entirely on your own with no inspiration. You may turn from one plan to another, uncertain which one is best. In the end you should find the opportunity to do what you desire, even though more planning and time will be needed. This is a busy month, much to do and a financial interest to be considered. Avoid impatience and do not allow emotional unrest to interfere with good common sense.

May—A Number Nine Personal Year

As the result of the practical arrangements of last

month, you should find yourself very busy, active in the midst of changes and undertakings you have been getting ready for during the past months. You may even be thrilled and excited over getting ready to experience new situations. This is a forward moving month and many circumstances will take place which will force you to move forward with spirit and enthusiasm. Even though plans are getting under way, everything may not be clear as to the outcome. Time is still a consideration. Go ahead determinedly. Keep in mind the fact that this month is the time to be up and doing and to make changes if you desire. This is only the springtime of the year, and life may not be able to bring about the final results until the fall of the year. Finals take more time. However, do not be hasty. Avoid quarrels, arguments, and disagreements, for they could upset and disrupt your well-laid plans. May could be very interesting, even exciting, with less responsibility and more expectations for personal freedom. You will see the way, although you may have some inner unrest or uncertainty, but this is the time to take action for the future if you have not already done so. The family, associates, and loved ones are part of the problem as you contemplate conditions. There is the possibility of some rearrangement of April's plans, but even so May is a good time to get things under way and moving forward.

June—A Number Nine Personal Year

From April to June you will be in a period of transition with a good many adjustments to make relative to others and the things of the past. You should become conscious of some of the rewards which the closing cycle promises and see some of the improvements you have expected, all mixed up with the past cycle's finals which have kept things moving slowly. Now and then the sense of futility I have spoken of may crop up because you are so anxious to know what to do. Time is still needed, for the tide has not yet fully turned, as there are affairs of the home and family which demand attention and time. There might even be a slight sacrifice necessary and it might be this very thing that finally shows the trend of events. At times during this year you may feel a lack of vitality. Keep your health up to par. A lot of responsibility rests on your shoulders. Many nice results run through this month for you, and you can receive help, money, and assistance in a nice way and through being kind, helpful, and sympathetic and not too self-determined. There is little to be gained all year long by trying to force an issue with anyone. Should you hurry results, even until September, it might cause delay later and you could realize disappointment and wish you had waited awhile. You have really accomplished a lot up to this time and deserve a reward, but at the same time the real personal satisfaction as to how things have turned out should be realized about now. It is possible, as this is your Number Nine Year and the closing of a cycle, that you will have moments when you will wonder if it is all worthwhile. To make the effort may seem futile to you only because you feel you have given so much. There is little to be gained by being emotional or by giving up.

There may be the culmination of a good many ways and means and possibly a change in situation or a person going out of your circle of activity. A need to help someone is present this month. This adjustment may be pleasing to you.

July—A Number Nine Personal Year

This is the sabbatical month of the year and you should find more time to be on your own, free from much of the duty and responsibility of the past few months. A good many things should be behind you as the result of the adjustment regarding home and property of last month. You may, surprisingly, feel alone and not sure of what you want to do. It would be well to take a trip to get away for awhile to gain a new outlook on future interests. While much has taken place to clear away the past, you are in an "in-between-time" and just what you personally are going to do is not fully on the boards. You will be deeply conscious in your mind and heart that you are done with someone or something. Deep conclusions about yourself and your life will flood your mind with much certainty. The way to the future and just what you want to do will still not fully show up, or at least you may realize you cannot act upon it right now. What you think about others, life in general, and for yourself, is likely to be changed when the way finally opens up, but that you are finished with something of no further value to you is in your mind. You should have interesting and unusual experiences this month through others, possibly strangers, but there should be a friend who will make things worth-while if you are helpful. You will feel sure that old contacts are at an end and that new interests are not too far off, but at this time rest, relaxation, study, and quiet thinking are the most important issues. Keep your own counsel and let others work out their own affairs. Health matters at this time need attention to avoid some moments of *low tide* later in the year. You may find that you are not up to your best effort, the reason you should take time out to loaf and rest, and to get away from people and the crowd for awhile. Have faith in yourself and life. This is the victory and the last test of the year. You may be very busy, too busy unless you deliberately take time out, and it is possible you may be torn between relatives and your own desires. What you do this month affects the fall of the year and the good which will come to you. Let go of anything that wants to get away. There is really nothing you need to be troubled about. Poise, inner calm, and spiritual attraction will take care of everything.

August—A Number Nine Personal Year

From now on move forward in an active way. You will feel more power to direct your affairs, finances, and relationships with others. There is a business influence present, and you are likely to be asked to give some of your time to consideration and analysis of a business opportunity or undertaking. This is likely to be temporary or just a plan, but is in the nature of a stepping stone to interests which are to be undertaken during the fall of the year, and may subtly affect the activities of the coming year. Others are concerned, too, and you may be doing as much to help them as to help yourself. Use good judgment; do not allow personal sentiment to affect this judgment. Be businesslike and take hold of your affairs. Tie up unfinished business or activities to clear the way for the future. The realization of a love affair or the love affairs of others may take your time or require your help and advice. Be wise enough not to become involved unless you are sure. Give advice, but do not mix in, for this is one of the times when you need to be strong, and even in your own emotional affairs be wise and sure of the foundation upon which you face the future. Put yourself into general business affairs and show your executive ability. You should have a reward of recognition and some honor this month.

From now on affairs seem to go forward in a more active way, and you should be able to control them better. This is a business month and you are apt to spend some time in analyzing business affairs relative to the future. Business undertakings may be a necessary stepping stone to help others as well as yourself. Papers and matters of a legal nature can come up again and should be adjusted for final settlement. Money may not be too easy but negotiations are going on. Many plans are present toward improvement and things concealed will be brought to light. Love affairs and business matters get mixed up, but little adjustments lead to clearer judgment and more efficient management for the future and for your own good.

September—A Number Nine Personal Year

You should find satisfaction in the results of your past efforts. A more hopeful outlook will begin to materialize now and you will discover sometime during this month what you have been seeking all year long. You can go ahead now with more determination and what you want to do should be clear and certain. However, for the next three months, the final months of the cycle, you may find that you are marking time, conscious of a few disappointments, or at least you might feel some sorrow for what you have given up or finished, even though the necessity was there. Life is now moving forward, and you should plan for the future and make ready to meet a new life, new interests, with a quickening of your ambitions; new opportunities and a new outlook on life are there now. You will be surprisingly emotional, and will do much thinking and remembering, but the past must be put behind you in order that the channel for the new may be open and clear. This has not been an *ordinary* year, but one of drama, feeling, color, experience, emotion of high potency that has required much of you in the way of understanding and giving. It has not been and is not now a time to be selfish or personal, for all things seem to shape up of their own accord and for the best as you keep the impersonal attitude of mind at all times. This has not been easy to do, but is still required of you in all your relationships.

October—A Number Nine Personal Year

During this month you will know what you are going

to do, and you should be busy about it in many ways. New interests, new associations, and something helpful and beneficial through others are present. You might even be in a different association or environment. This is a new start mentally, something to do or learn which is different but interesting. It is possible you may also be marking time, while plans are developing, because others have something to say or are in charge. You must cooperate willingly during this time. You will still need to give time to keeping well and rested, for this year of emotion and finals will take a lot of your energy. All these finals are nothing to worry about and may be only small considerations, but the test is in your own spiritual growth, your compassion, understanding, and willingness to do mental, material, and spiritual house-cleaning so that you may move forward fresh and alert into the new cycle. Enjoy life and prepare quietly for the future until the time of the new year in January. Next year will be just the opposite from this year. This year, life takes hold, but next year you must take hold and get things done, so enjoy the remainder of this year. Right now, mutual benefit is the keynote of the month, giving and receiving from others or someone in particular. This year should end with special interests, and on the whole be very good. You may have to take a stand, but someone can help you, and during this fall you should find help and mutual interest with someone else, for while you are clear in mind about yourself and what you want to do, you may have to mark time or help someone else to get just what *you* want. Something not fully anticipated can be present this month and good, too. A few annoyances, but take care of them patiently.

November—A Number Nine Personal Year

This month should find you busy in many ways. An interesting month in association with others. You may even be dependent upon others to help you while you wait for time to clear the way. Your health or the health needs of others take some of your time now. You will probably spend time getting information relative to what you want to do later or sizing up the situation to find out what you want or how much you want it. Take this month patiently and without nervousness; and quietly hold to your plans and desires, even though it may seem to you that your patience is tested by others trying to force you against your will. This is simply because the end of the closing year of this cycle is interesting but lacks positive force with which to drive plans forward. There is much going on under the surface, and time will tell. November should be generally pleasant. Others depend upon you a lot. There may be a little waiting, but someone helping or sharing your interests could be of help to both. You will be marking time, but will be busy in spite of some delay. You may meet old friends and renew old acquaintances. There is much to your advantage through cooperation now.

December—A Number Nine Personal Year

This is really a vacation month, a time to do pleasant things. It is the last month before you must get busy. Entertain others, spend enough money to give you the feeling of personal importance and enjoyment of life, youth, and living, but not with extravagance or foolish impulse. If you desire to take a trip for change or fun, do so, but join with friends for a generally happy Christmas. Be creative and constructive and help others to enjoy life. Something will be different, or you may feel that you are alone or not in your usual activities, but this will be of your own doing, so it is not a problem, and there is so much to gain in the way of friendship and pleasure that you will be pleasantly busy and in some way inspired by what you are doing. An opportunity may present itself for you to express your talents and ability in a nice way. Talk, conversation, lectures, letters prove interesting. Talk a lot too, and have fun, but do not say too much about your future plans at this time. An opportunity is present to advance through your talents and artistic ability and along the lines of your career, and by this time, just before you open your new cycle of experience, you should be ready to take a step toward a more permanent plan for building your future, now that so much is cleared up and settled. A mixture of feelings may be present during the holidays, but others will be nice to you, friendships should prove helpful, and you may enjoy the setup very much.

Advice to Counsellors

ADVICE TO COUNSELLORS

Building A Clientele

Clients who have been helped by your advice and sympathetic understanding of their personal problems, as revealed by their Right Action numbers, will consult you again and again. It may be to give you a report; or to talk things over again; or a new problem has come up; or perhaps, to have their Right Action advice for another year; even to test your ability as a Numerologist.

It is advisable to send an announcement or brochure from time to time, or at the beginning of the new year. Your client will appreciate it and feel more sure of your work as a counsellor, with mutual respect.

Monthly Advice

Even though you have given your client a complete Right Action analysis for the present personal year, many men and women feel the need of personal direction, month by month. They like to receive advice and direction for each month. An office practice can be built up in this way, by appointment, brochure or cassette.

Note: It is *important*—that *you*, as a counsellor understand and use the following chart for a clear concept of the trend of events as they begin and end each year, within a nine-year major cycle.

INTERPRETING THE COUNSELLOR'S CHART

A Nine-Year Cycle of Personal Years

Presenting the interplay of cycles of nine during each personal year.

During the first five years, a full cycle of nine is never fully worked out.

During the sixth year, one cycle is finished, another not fully developed.

During the seventh year, two cycles are begun, only one fully developed.

Notice the *sudden completion* of a cycle in *January of the Eight Personal Year.*

Again in the Nine Personal Year, two cycles are begun, only one completed.

During the Four, Five, and Six Personal Years, the Seven is faced twice.

During the Three Personal Year, Number Six is repeated twice.

During the Four and Five Personal Years, Number Six is repeated twice.

All these should be kept in mind in answering important business and domestic questions.

Again, observe that the numbers of the months of *January* and *February* of the next year are the same as the numbers of the months of *November* and *December* of the year before. However, *and this is important,* the numbers of each *Personal Year* are quite different. A change of thought, plans, methods, or way of approaching new plans must be considered, as the new year is entered into. This accounts for the delays in getting started and often why some of the work or plans for the next year may need to be slightly changed after the planning of November and December of each year.

Counsellor's Chart

Calendar Months		Personal Years 1—2—3—4—5—6—7—8—9
January	-1	2—3—4—5—6—7—8—9—1
February	-2	3—4—5—6—7—8—9—1—2
March	-3	4—5—6—7—8—9—1—2—3
April	-4	5—6—7—8—9—1—2—3—4
May	-5	6—7—8—9—1—2—3—4—5
June	-6	7—8—9—1—2—3—4—5—6
July	-7	8—9—1—2—3—4—5—6—7
August	-8	9—1—2—3—4—5—6—7—8
September	-9	1—2—3—4—5—6—7—8—9
October	-1	2—3—4—5—6—7—8—9—1
November	-2	3—4—5—6—7—8—9—1—2
December	-3	4—5—6—7—8—9—1—2—3

Reduce the calendar month October 10 to 1 November 11 to 2 December 12 to 3

These months have more force than the single numbered months.

An Occult Interpretation of Numbers*

Number One
A path cut straight and level along difficult lines. With proper apprehension and caution there will be good fortune. Capable of interpreting and executing the most difficult things. Gaining fuller understanding of life.

Number Two
Exercising forbearance. Fashions after the course of heaven and earth. That which is in a state of repose and freedom.

Number Three
Patience and obedience will bring success. Seeking after strange objects too much may change the course of the whole life.

Number Four
Should blunt the sharp points and unravel the complications. Bring one's self into agreement with others.

----

*From THE FUNDAMENTAL PRINCIPLES OF YI KING, TAO, Cabbalas of Egypt and the Hebrews, by Veolita Parke Boyle. Published in 1929, Occult Publishing Company, Chicago.

Direct all advantages into a single course, then ten times success.

Number Five
Firmness is necessary for success. Fail to express opinions on unfamiliar subjects. Discrimination. Respect jurisprudence.

Number Six
Quieting others. Can make muddy waters clear. Giving honors to others. All movement directed by order.

Number Seven
Causes others to forget their poverty. Seeks the solitude of own mind. Revelation concerning occult means. High office the result of experience. Nourishes and educates the people.

Number Eight
Represents the union of many and how it is to be attained. Choose virtuous associations. Believes in that which secures the best order.

Number Nine
Sincere in promises. Pardons easily. Heals the souls of others. Integrity. Faithful minister. Benevolence. Weighs matters well. Rich in resources.